MODELING AND COMPUTER SIMULATION

Edited by **Dragan Cvetković**

Modeling and Computer Simulation
http://dx.doi.org/10.5772/intechopen.73381
Edited by Dragan Cvetković

Contributors

Vojtech Merunka, Graciano Dieck-Assad, Antonio Favela-Contreras, José Luis Vega-Fonseca, Isaías Hernández-Ramírez, Sevcan Emek, Şebnem Bora, Ivana Dragan Cvetkovic, Misa Stojicevic, Branislav Popkonstantinovic, Dragan Mladen Cvetković

First published in London, United Kingdom, 2019 by IntechOpen
IntechOpen is the global imprint of INTECHOPEN LIMITED, registered in England and Wales, registration number: 11086078, The Shard, 25th floor, 32 London Bridge Street
London, SE19SG – United Kingdom
Printed in Croatia

British Library Cataloguing-in-Publication Data
A catalogue record for this book is available from the British Library

Additional hard copies can be obtained from orders@intechopen.com

Modeling and Computer Simulation, Edited by Dragan Cvetković
p. cm.
Print ISBN 978-1-78985-795-5
Online ISBN 978-1-78985-796-2

For EU product safety concerns:
IN TECH d.o.o., Prolaz Marije Krucifikse Kozulić 3, 51000 Rijeka, Croatia,
info@intechopen.com or visit our website at intechopen.com.

Meet the editor

Dragan Cvetković graduated in aeronautics from the Faculty of Mechanical Engineering, University of Belgrade, in 1988. In the Aeronautical Department, he defended his doctoral dissertation in December 1997. So far, he has published 63 books, scripts, and practicums about computers and computer programs, aviation weapons, and flight mechanics. He has published a large number of scientific papers in Serbia and abroad as well.
From 2007 to 2013, he worked as an assistant professor and from October 1, 2013, he has been working as the dean of the Faculty of Informatics and Computing both at the Singidunum University, Belgrade. He became a full professor in the field of Informatics and Computing in March 2014.

Contents

Preface

Information technologies have changed people's lives to a great extent, and now it is almost impossible to imagine any activity that does not depend on computers in some way. Since the invention of the first computer systems, people have been trying to use computers to solve complex problems in various areas. The need for computer systems for the calculation of different building and automotive constructions has appeared with the development of . Traditional methods of calculation have been replaced by computer programs that have the ability to predict the behaviour of structures under different loading conditions. Hence, expensive experiments, tests, and examinations have been replaced by cheaper and more powerful computational methods that do not require the destruction of structures to determine their capacity.

Fortunately, computer programs allow such problems to be easily solved. Computer simulation or a computer model has the task of simulating the behaviour of an abstract model of a particular system. Computer simulations have become a useful part of mathematical of many natural systems in physics, quantum mechanics, chemistry, biology, economic systems, psychology, and social sciences, as well as in the engineering process of new technologies to gain better insight into their way of working and behaving.

Computer simulations are different from computer programs. Contrary to computer programs that run for a few minutes, simulations can be run on a local network and can last for hours or even days.

Nowadays, computer simulations are used to solve problems in all spheres of life. Meteorological forecasts, the calculation of rainfall, water flows in rivers, underground water flows, and oil exploitation are just some of the areas that cannot be imagined without computers. One of the most interesting computer applications is the simulation of processes in the human body. Modern software solutions enable the calculation of muscle fatigue in certain activities, the deposition of fat in blood vessels, the risk of cancer, etc. In the future, these programs will be able to allow the realization of virtual surgeries and to predict the effects of surgeries before they are performed in reality.

The chapters are listed in a logical order, but they can be arranged differently, depending on the point of view.

The first chapter illustrates the advantages and disadvantages of computer simulations and their applications in almost every area and environment of everyday life.

The second chapter describes a modeling methodology to provide the main characteristics of a simulation tool for the analysis of the steady-state, transient operation and control of steam generation processes, such as heat recovery steam generators.

In the third chapter, the authors describe how to develop an agent-based model and simulation for biological systems in the Repast Simphony platform, which is a Java-based modeling system. Agent-based modeling and simulation are powerful techniques for simulating and exploring phenomena that include a large set of active components represented by agents.

The fourth chapter deals with 3D modeling and assembling of all escapement parts of Thomas Earnshaw's chronometer. First, the constructive geometry of mechanisms was completed. Then, computer simulation was accomplished in the program "SolidWorks 2016," which generated simulation results that appeared to be very close to the real ones.

The fifth chapter presents the original computer-aided organizational modeling and simulation of relevant sociotechnical processes with regard to new housing and building law and regional management trends in the European Union.

I would like to express my sincere gratitude to all the authors and coauthors for their contributions. The successful completion of this book has been the result of the cooperation of many people. Especially, I would like to thank the Publishing Process Manager Ms. Jasna Božić for her support during the publishing process.

Dragan Cvetković
Singidunum University
Faculty of Informatics and Computing
Belgrade, Republic of Serbia

Chapter 1

Introductory Chapter: Computer Simulation

Dragan Cvetković

Additional information is available at the end of the chapter

http://dx.doi.org/10.5772/intechopen.84198

1. Introduction

Information technologies have changed people's lives to a great extent, so it is almost impossible to imagine any activity which does not depend on computers. Once the first computer systems appeared, people were trying to take advantage of computers in order to solve complex problems in various areas. With the development of industry, demands for computers and computational programs in structural analysis have evolved. Traditional methods of constructing are replaced by computer programs that have the ability to predict the behavior of structures under different load conditions [1, 2]. Thus, expensive experiments, tests, and examinations are substituted by cheaper and more powerful computational methods that do not require the destruction of the structure itself in order to determine its capacity.

1.1. Process of modeling and making of reliable computer model

Computer programs help in solving this kind of problems. Firstly, the simulation of the real system should be made, and after that, if the simulation gives satisfactory results, realization of previously examined system can be carried out. Computer simulation or a computer model has the task to simulate an abstract model of a particular or equivalent system. Computer simulations have become a useful part of mathematical modeling of many natural systems in physics, mechanics, chemistry, biology, economic systems, psychology, and social sciences, as well as in all branches of engineering, in order to gain a better insight into the work of previously mentioned systems [1, 3, 4].

In order to have a useful model, it is necessary to determine its behavior for defined and limited set of variables. This means that for some random input parameters are observed corresponding output values.

1.2. Computer modeling and computer simulation

Simulation in everyday life can be related to various activities. If this word is used in the computer technology, then the term simulation represents the process of creating the abstract system models from the real environment and carrying out the appropriate number of experiments on them. When the experiments are carried out on a computer, then they are named computer modeling and computer simulation (**Figure 1**).

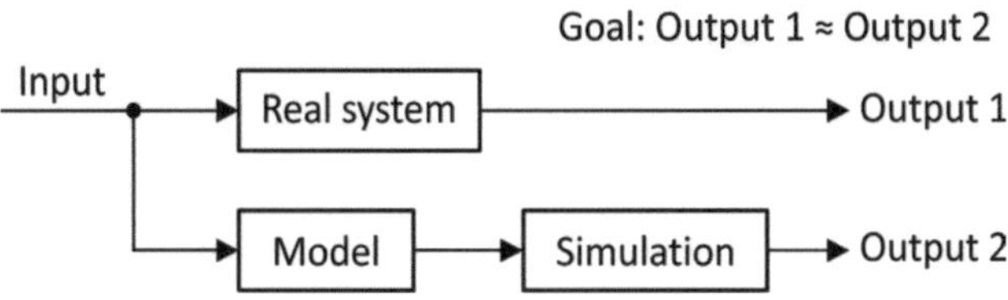

Figure 1. Link between real system modeling and computer simulation.

The input data vary and depend on many factors when the models and simulations are taken into consideration. For example, some models require very simple inputs (e.g., the input for the simulation of an AC sinusoid is based on few numbers), while other models require terabytes of input data (e.g., simulation of weather or climate changes).

Input data are provided by various devices which are:

- Sensors and other physical devices that are connected to the model
- Control panel that directly affect the progress of the simulation itself in some way
- Current or older data brought in manually
- The values that represent the output products from other processes or operations
- Values that represent output elements of other models or simulations

It should be noted that the systems that receive data from external sources must be "careful": they should know what these data represent and to which elements are actually connected. The precision must be taken into account and the errors should not occur. If the errors appear, they should be reduced to the minimum. The mathematics integrated in the computer is not perfect, so the approximate results, result abbreviations, or neutralization of small errors can lead to an increase of potential errors. It is necessary, in some cases, to analyze the resulting error in order to verify that the simulation output is valid and that it can be used in further calculations and simulations. Even small errors in the original input data can accumulate in significant errors in further simulations [1, 4, 5].

1.3. Why do we need computer modeling and computer simulations?

What do we use modeling and simulation for? Are they necessary? These questions are asked very often, and there are plenty of reasons for their creation and usage, and the most important are the following ones:

- It is impossible to determine the analytical solution of the analytical model.
- The system is too complex and it is impossible to describe it analytically.
- The experiment within a real system or the experiment on the real system is, in most cases, either unprofitable or too complex. Modeling and simulation can show whether a further investment in the experiment is justified or not.
- Often the aim of modeling and simulation is to perceive the functionality of the existing real system, whose structure is barely known or cannot be approached to.
- When the optimal or optimized functioning of a system is needed, it is necessary to change various parameters. If the real system is taken into account, this is often impossible because there is no such a system. In other words, that kind of a system has not been built yet, or the prices of such an experiment are excessive. In such situations, modeling and simulation are the best solutions.
- Sometimes it is necessary to simulate the conditions that lead to the destruction of the system. The destruction of the real system, in most cases, is not allowed, so the computer simulation, in such situations, is the only solution.
- When it comes to long-term processes of real system or within the real system, then time can be a problematic factor. In such situations, computer simulation can "accelerate" the process and shorten it artificially.
- When it comes to extremely fast processes of the real system or within the real system, computer simulation is a solution which allows the monitoring of high-speed processes gradually or slowly. This is very important, since it is not possible in real life or in real environment.
- Sometimes the experiment should be stopped for various reasons, and it is often impossible in real terms. When it comes to computer simulation of such an experiment, there is no problem, because the simulation can be stopped and continued when it is necessary.

1.4. Advantages and disadvantages of computer simulations

Like everything in life, computer simulations are not perfect and there are different problems. Simulations are, generally speaking, very useful, but they have advantages as well as disadvantages. The basic advantages of computer simulations are:

- When a model is created, then it can be used repeatedly for the analysis of required process, structures, and similar elements.
- Computer simulations can be extremely helpful, even if the input data are incomplete and with a certain amount of arbitrariness.
- In most cases it is easier and cheaper to get the output data of the simulation than the output data of the real system.
- Computer simulation generates the necessary data that can be used for the evaluation and assessment of any system characteristic and without big restrictions.

- In some cases, the computer simulation may be the only way to resolve the problems appropriately.
- Computer simulation can describe and solve complex problems by using dynamic random variables, which are unavailable in mathematical modeling.

The major disadvantages of computer simulations are:

- Making of simulation models as well as computer simulations can be expensive and time consuming (it refers to the time needed for their development, testing, and verification).
- By using computer simulations, neither the relation between output and input variables nor optimal solutions can be obtained.
- Knowledge of different tools and methods is required for the development and use of simulation models and computer simulations as well.
- Model evaluation is quite a complex process and requires additional experimentation in different environments.

No matter what, computer simulation is a very useful thing, and its use is rapidly increasing in environments and situations where it is possible. Obviously, the application of computer simulation has many more advantages than disadvantages, and it is certain that computer simulations are going to be dominant in almost every area and environment of everyday life [4, 6].

Author details

Dragan Cvetković

Address all correspondence to: dcvetkovic@singidunum.ac.rs

Faculty of Informatics and Computing, Singidunum University, Belgrade, Republic of Serbia

References

[1] Steinhauser MO. Computer Simulation in Physics and Engineering. Berlin: De Gruyter; 2012

[2] Mityushev V, Nawalaniec W, Rylko N. Introduction to Mathematical Modeling and Computer Simulation. 1st ed. USA: Chapman and Hall/CRC; 2018

[3] Goldman R. An Integrated Introduction to Computer Graphics and Geometric Modeling. 1st ed. USA: CRC Press; 2009

[4] Law AM. Simulation Modeling and Analysis. 5th ed. USA: McGraw-Hill Education; 2014

[5] Zeigler B, Muzy A, Kofman E. Theory of Modeling and Simulation—Discrete Event & Iterative System Computational Foundations. USA: Academic Press; 2018

[6] Shiflet AB, Shiflet GW. Introduction to Computational Science: Modeling and Simulation for the Sciences. 2nd ed. USA: Princeton University Press; 2014

Chapter 2

Modeling, Simulation, and Control of Steam Generation Processes

Graciano Dieck-Assad, José Luis Vega-Fonseca,
Isaías Hernández-Ramírez and
Antonio Favela-Contreras

Additional information is available at the end of the chapter

http://dx.doi.org/10.5772/intechopen.79410

Abstract

This chapter describes a modeling methodology to provide the main characteristics of a simulation tool to analyze the steady state, transient operation, and control of steam generation processes, such as heat recovery steam generators (HRSG). The methodology includes a modular strategy that considers individual heat exchangers such as: economizers, evaporators, superheaters, drum tanks, and control systems. The modular strategy consists of the development of a numerical modeling tool that integrates sub-models based upon first principle equations of mass, energy, and momentum balance. The main heat transfer mechanisms characterize the dynamics of steam generation systems during normal and abnormal operations, which include the response of key process variables such as vapor pressure, temperature, and mass flow rate. Other important variables are: gas temperature, fluid temperature, drum pressure, drum's liquid level, and mass flow rate at each module. Those variables are usually analyzed with design predicted performance of real industrial equipment such as HRSG systems. Finally, two case studies of the application of the modeling strategy are provided to show the effectiveness and utility of the methodology.

Keywords: steam generation, modeling methodology, first principle equations, heat recovery steam generators (HRSG), boiler modeling, economizer, superheater, heat exchange surfaces, heat exchanger

1. Introduction

Electric energy production and conservation has become a key technological challenge in the development of nations to promote their steady and healthy socioeconomic development. Also,

the new technological developments to support Industry 4.0 and Internet of Things (IoT) require the solution of medium scale system models to optimize the performance of energy sources remotely by the incorporation of site-specific performance indices Ref [1–6]. Nowadays, the most common electric energy production process uses heat exchangers to transfer their calorific energy from flue gases to water-vapor that impinge prime movers connected to electric generators. The gas turbine is one of the best option in quick load following combined cycle power units due to their low costs in initial investment, operation, low emissions, and low reaction time or response time in generating electric energy from scratch. In this case, two-third of the mechanical work is used to self-power the operation of the turbine system and the rest can be used to generate electric energy. This characteristic produces an estimated efficiency between 25 and 45% [1] in gas turbine systems. Thermal and energetic engineering has developed methods to increase the efficiency in energy generation processes such that residues of a particular process can be used to drive another heat exchange process, and therefore, this technique is called cogeneration. The most common cogeneration technique takes advantage of the residual heat of a gas turbine to produce useful thermal energy loaded to vapor or heated air, and then, this energy is used in other industrial processes to increase electric energy production.

An example of vapor production uses a heat recovery steam generator (HRSG). **Figure 1** shows a HRSG and its components, where the inlet illustrates the hot gases coming from the gas turbine. The hot or flue gases transfer heat to different tube banks driving water as the working fluid and its pressure and temperature increase until reaching the required operating predicted performance conditions. This chapter discusses a methodology to develop and simulate models of steam generation processes in steady state and transient conditions from the stand point of thermos-hydraulics. The methodology can produce good simulation tools to evaluate system operation in startup, shutdown, stand by, and load changes during useful

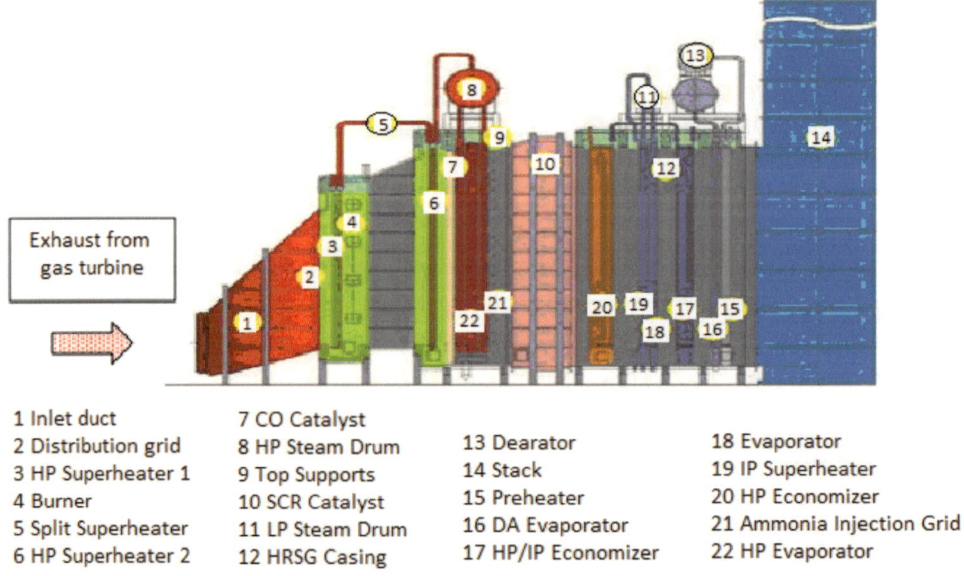

Figure 1. Example of a horizontal HRSG [2, 3] in energy transfer processes.

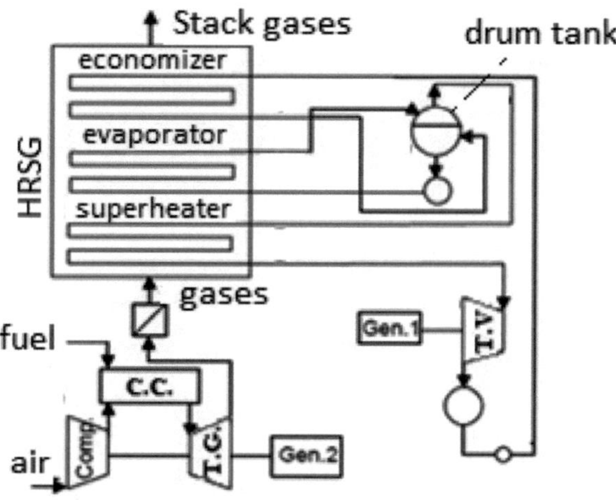

Figure 2. Modular strategy in modeling a steam generation system [4].

equipment life. Examples of modeling efforts are discussed with basic configuration of boiler furnaces and HRSG that includes economizer, evaporator, and super-heater modules. Moreover, the methodology proposes a modular approach strategy such as the one depicted in **Figure 2**.

The technical literature shows models that permit the evaluation of transient processes in boilers and vapor generators. Those models are based in first principle thermo-hydraulic equations and some of the most important ones are discussed as follows. Mansour [4] studies the prediction of transient behaviors of combined cycle gas turbine (CCGT) plants and describes mathematical models of the dynamic behavior of the main components in the combined cycle process. His study describes the heat transfer equations of superheater, evaporator, and economizer that allow him to develop a numerical model and simulation system. His results are validated with field measurements from a power unit in Egypt. Dumont [5] describes models for HRSG in boilers "once-through" without drums. The economizer, superheater, and evaporator models are lumped in one complex main super-model, which is complex and difficult to differentiate individual component output variables. Dieck-Assad [6, 7] presents the development of a boiler model departing from first principle equations. This chapter adopts methodologies used in [6, 7] to model drum-evaporator systems considering specific modular control volumes and state variables that describe the dynamics of the energy transfer process from flue gases to the working fluid.

2. Modeling methodology

The first principle equations used to develop a steam generation process model require simplifications and assumptions that limit the scope and application for which the model is created. Also, if control system optimization is desired, a performance index is defined and the accuracy predictions should be within tolerances defined by the amount of improvements expected by the original application goals.

For instance, a HRSG consists of a tandem of heat exchangers such that their mathematical modeling uses the governing equations from heat transfer, fluid dynamics thermal properties of tube materials, and thermal properties of water. The heat exchange physical phenomena involve nonlinear models that produce complex equation systems to represent a typical heat exchange process. In predicting the steady state and transient operation, the governing equations require a set of assumptions and considerations such as:

- The hot (flue) gases inertia is neglected.
- Heat loss around a heat exchanger control volume is not considered.
- The combustion gases flow has a uniform homogeneous distribution across the tube interchange area.
- The combustion gases coming from the turbine are considered to behave ideal at a pressure of 1 atm.
- The tubes in a distributed arrangement are identical, in other words, the water-vapor mass flow rate divides among the number of tubes leaving the header and the quantity of flue gases between tubes is the same.
- The following considerations are made at each module: at the economizer, the water flowing is at saturated liquid conditions, in the evaporator, we assume two phases at saturated conditions, and in the superheater, only superheated steam is considered except for the control volume of the attemperator system.

2.1. Heat exchangers

The gas flow coming from the turbine has also a pressure loss through the heat exchange process, however, this work focus on the internal behavior of the heat exchange fluid, and therefore, the velocity, pressure, and composition of flue gases are the same as the entering conditions to the first module. The superheater and economizer are considered as large heat exchangers where the flue gas follows trajectories similar to the ones shown in **Figure 3**. The water flows through a series of tube banks, which are aligned in normal directions to hot gases flow coming from the turbine. The tube banks are parallel among them and they are tied together with U tube connections as shown in **Figure 3**.

Figure 4 shows the traversal view of the tube bank heat exchange structure. This traversal view is composed by small control volumes represented in **Figure 5**. The energy equations in the x-y plane for gas, water, and metal have been reported in [4] and they are shown as follows.

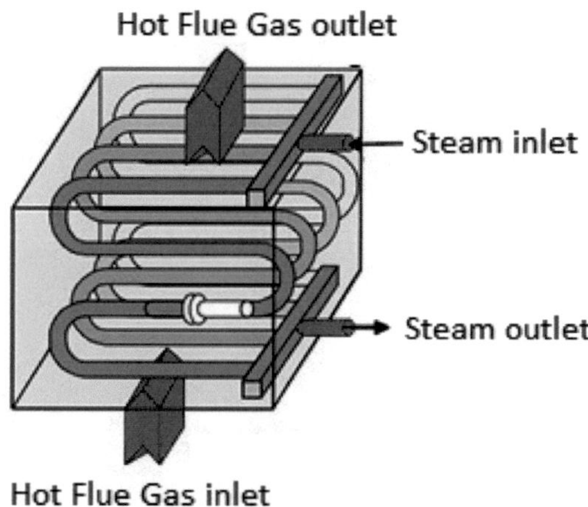

Figure 3. Multistage crossing flow heat exchange structure for economizer and superheater [4].

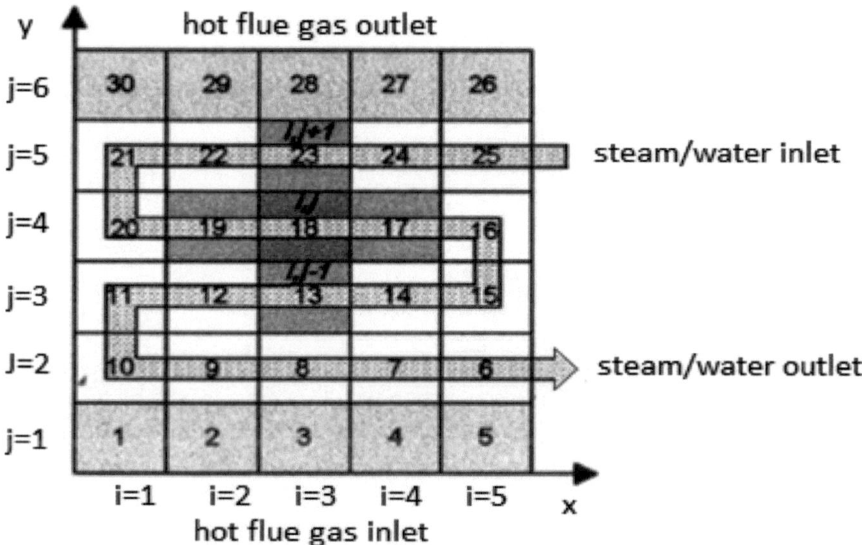

Figure 4. Traversal view representation of a heat exchange surface control volumes at modules of typical heat transfer tube surface (Plane x-y) [4]

For gas:

$$\frac{\partial T_g}{\partial t} + \gamma u_g \frac{\partial T_g}{\partial y} = -\frac{\dot{Q}_{gm}}{\rho_g V_g c_v} + \frac{\lambda_g}{\rho_g c_v}\left(\frac{\partial^2 T_g}{\partial y^2}\right) \tag{1}$$

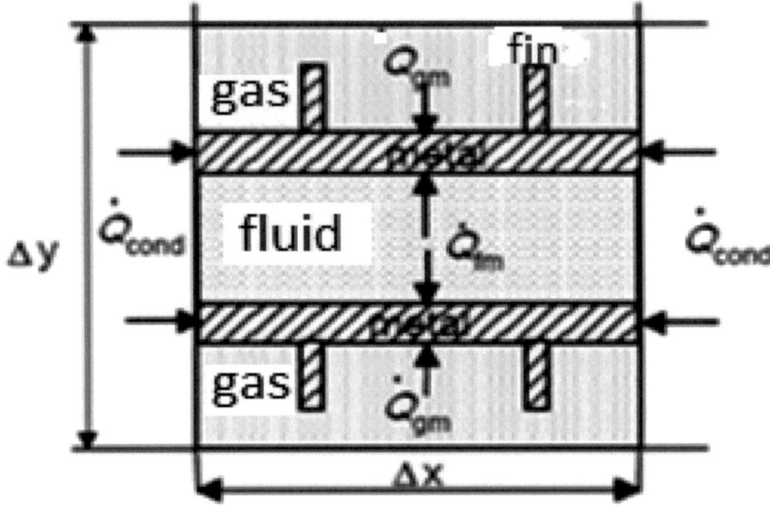

Figure 5. Control volume representation numerical meshes modules in typical heat transfer surfaces [4].

For water:

$$\frac{\partial T_f}{\partial t}+u_f\frac{\partial T_f}{\partial x}=-\frac{\dot{Q}_{fm}}{\rho_f V_f c_p}+\frac{\lambda_f}{\rho_f c_p}\left(\frac{\partial^2 T_f}{\partial x^2}\right) \tag{2}$$

For metal:

$$\frac{\partial T_m}{\partial t}=\frac{\dot{Q}_{gm}+\dot{Q}_{fm}}{\rho_m V_m c_m}+\frac{\lambda_m}{\rho_m c_m}\left(\frac{\partial^2 T_m}{\partial x^2}\right) \tag{3}$$

Every tube element is treated as a system group due to the fact that the Biot number (the ratio between the conduction heat transfer to convection heat transfer over the body surface) is less than 0.1. The rate of heat transfer from the hot flue gases to the metal tube is:

$$\dot{Q}_{gm}=A_o h_{gm}\left(T_g-T_m\right) \tag{4}$$

The rate of heat transfer from the tube walls to the internal fluid (water/steam) is determined as follows:

$$\dot{Q}_{fm}=A_i h_{fm}\left(T_f-T_m\right) \tag{5}$$

Eqs. (1) and (3) describe the heat transfer mechanism between the tube banks for the heat exchanger and have the characteristic of a parabolic partial differential equation. In order to discretize the equations, the back in time implicit Euler's center space (BTCS) method was selected. This method is very stable both in time and space, and the step sizes in time and space have no restrictions to assure a good solution [5]. This method approximates the partial differential equation with finite differences between points as illustrated in **Figure 6**, where "t" is time step and "i" is the space step.

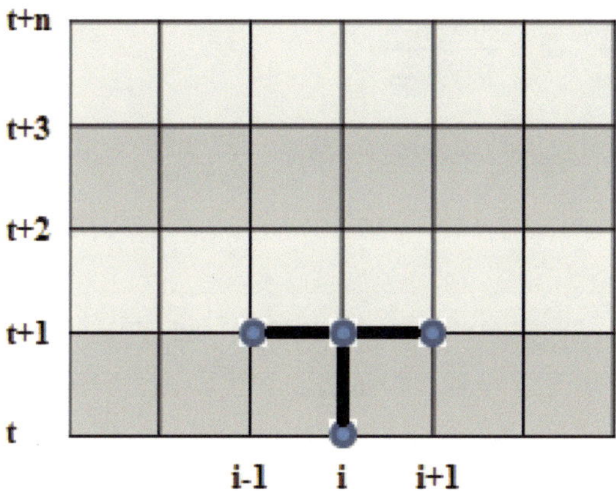

Figure 6. Scheme for the BTCS implicit method [5].

This way, an approximation to the partial differential equation is reached by finite differences, where each partial term of Eqs. (1)–(3) is represented by:

$$\frac{\partial \theta}{\partial \varphi} = \frac{\theta_i^{t+1} - \theta_i^t}{\Delta\theta} \frac{\partial \theta}{\partial \varphi} = \frac{\theta_i^{t+1} - \theta_i^t}{\Delta\theta} \tag{6}$$

$$\frac{\partial^2 \theta}{\partial \varphi^2} = \frac{\theta_{i-1}^{t+1} - 2\theta_i^{t+1} + \theta_{i+1}^{t+1}}{\Delta\theta^2} \frac{\partial^2 \theta}{\partial \varphi^2} = \frac{\theta_{i-1}^{t+1} - 2\theta_i^{t+1} + \theta_{i+1}^{t+1}}{\Delta\theta^2} \tag{7}$$

where θ represents any of the properties and ϕ any of the parameters.

Using the tube representation of **Figure 4** and establishing the numerical mesh from **Figure 5**, the following algebraic equations describe the heat transfer at the tube Banks:

- For flue gas

$$T_{g,i,j}^{t} = -bT_{g,i,j-1}^{t+1} + a_p T_{g,i,j}^{t+1} - aT_{g,i,j+1}^{t+1} - sT_{m,i,j}^{t+1} \tag{8}$$

where,

$$a = \frac{\lambda_g \Delta t \Delta x}{\rho_g c_v V_g} \quad b = \frac{\lambda_g \Delta t \Delta x}{\rho_g c_v V_e} + \frac{\gamma \dot{m}_g \Delta t}{\rho_g V_e N_x N_r}$$
$$s = \frac{A_o h_{gm} \Delta t}{\rho_g V_g c_v} \quad a_p = 1 + a + b + s \quad s = \frac{A_o h_{gm} \Delta t}{\rho_g V_g c_v} \quad a_p = 1 + a + b + s \tag{9}$$

- For metal

$$\begin{gathered} T_{m,i,j}^{t} = -aT_{m,i-1,j}^{t+1} + a_p T_{m,i,j}^{t+1} - aT_{m,i+1,j}^{t+1} - bT_{g,i,j}^{t+1} - sT_{f,i,j}^{t+1} \\ T_{m,i,j}^{t} = -aT_{m,i-1,j}^{t+1} + a_p T_{m,i,j}^{t+1} - aT_{m,i+1,j}^{t+1} - bT_{g,i,j}^{t+1} - sT_{f,i,j}^{t+1} \end{gathered} \tag{10}$$

where,

$$a = \frac{\lambda_m \Delta t \Delta y}{\rho_m c_m V_m} \quad b = \frac{A_o h_{gm} \Delta t}{\rho_m V_m c_m}$$
$$s = \frac{A_i h_{fm} \Delta t}{\rho_m V_m c_m} \quad a_p = 1 + 2a + b + s\, s = \frac{A_i h_{fm} \Delta t}{\rho_m V_m c_m} \quad a_p = 1 + 2a + b + s \tag{11}$$

- Water/vapor

$$T_{f,i,j}^{t} = -bT_{f,i-1,j}^{t+1} + a_p T_{f,i,j}^{t+1} - aT_{f,i+1,j}^{t+1} - sT_{m,i,j}^{t+1} \tag{12}$$
$$T_{f,i,j}^{t} = -bT_{f,i-1,j}^{t+1} + a_p T_{f,i,j}^{t+1} - aT_{f,i+1,j}^{t+1} - sT_{m,i,j}^{t+1}$$

where,

$$a = \frac{\lambda_f \Delta t D_i}{\rho_f c_p V_f} \quad b = \frac{\lambda_f \Delta t D_i}{\rho_f c_p V_f} + \frac{\dot{m}_f \Delta t}{\rho_f V_f N_t}$$
$$s = \frac{A_i h_{fm} \Delta t}{\rho_f V_f c_p} \quad a_p = 1 + a + b + s \tag{13}$$

Ordering the algebraic representation of those equations for each of the discretization points, we can obtain a tri-diagonal matrix, which is solved using a standard Gauss elimination algorithm [8]. Therefore, this procedure allows us to evaluate the temperature behavior of the tube bank at each time step, in other words, its transient behavior.

The heat transfer coefficient between the flue gas and the tube bank structure is obtained using the Zukauskas correlation [9] as follows:

$$h_{gm} = \frac{\lambda}{D_o} E * B * Re^{C} * Pr_g^{D} h_{gm} = \frac{\lambda}{D_o} E * B * Re^{C} * Pr_g^{D} \tag{14}$$

where the coefficients B, C, and D are calculated according to the Reynolds number as described in **Table 1**.

where the Reynolds number is evaluated under maximum velocity conditions between tubes:

$$V_{max} = \frac{Pt}{Pt - D_o} V V_{max} = \frac{Pt}{Pt - D_o} V \tag{15}$$

In the case of heat transfer between the tube walls and the water/vapor fluid, we can use the Dittus-Boelter correlation for convection heat transfer as follows:

$$h_{fm} = 0.023 \frac{\lambda}{D_i} Re^{4/5} Pr^{n} \tag{16}$$
$$h_{fm} = 0.023 \frac{\lambda}{D_i} Re^{4/5} Pr^{n}$$

where n = 0.4 when the tube is at higher temperature than the working fluid (cooling) and n = 0.33 when the tube is at lower temperature than the working fluid (heating).

Staggered arrangement							
Reynolds		B		C		D	
10–500		1.04		0.4		0.36	
1000–200,000 (Pt/Pl < 2)		0.35(Pt/Pl)^0.2		0.5		0.36	
1000–200,000 (Pt/Pl > 2)		0.4		0.6		0.36	
>200,000		0.022		0.84		0.36	
Line arrangement							
Reynolds		B		C		D	
0.4–4		0.89		0.330		1/3	
4–40		0.911		0.385		1/3	
40–4000		0.683		0.466		1/3	
4000–40,000		0.193		0.618		1/3	
40,000–400,000		0.0266		0.805		1/3	
E Coefficient	N_{beds}->	1	2	3	4	5	
Line		0.7	0.8	0.9	0.9	0.9	1.0
Staggered		0.64	0.8	0.8	0.9	0.9	1.0

Table 1. Coefficients for the Zukauskas correlation [9].

2.2. Thermodynamic properties

The thermo-physical properties of the working fluids and flue gases that participate in heat exchange processes change with respect to temperature and pressure. Therefore, the thermodynamics properties model describes the water/vapor and hot gases behavior at different temperatures. The International Association of Properties of Water and Vapor, IAPWS, [10] proposes equations distributed in regions of thermodynamic state as illustrated in the pressure (p) versus temperature (T) diagram shown in **Figure 7**.

The simulation model integrates routines for the water thermodynamic properties, which are based and published in IAPWS-IF97 [10], "Release on the IAPWS Industrial Formulation 1997 for the Thermodynamic Properties of Water and Steam". For the thermodynamic properties of turbine waste gases, one can use the polynomials published by Yaws [11], which describe the behavior of each component in terms of temperature.

The heat transfer capacity in the tube banks is determined by the thermal conductivity, specific heat and density, which depend upon the operating temperature of the material. The ASME in "2001 ASME Boiler and Pressure Bessel Code, Section II – Materials" [12] describes and classifies the materials, which have similar behavior due to their chemical composition and their thermodynamic properties are shown as a function of the working temperature [13–15].

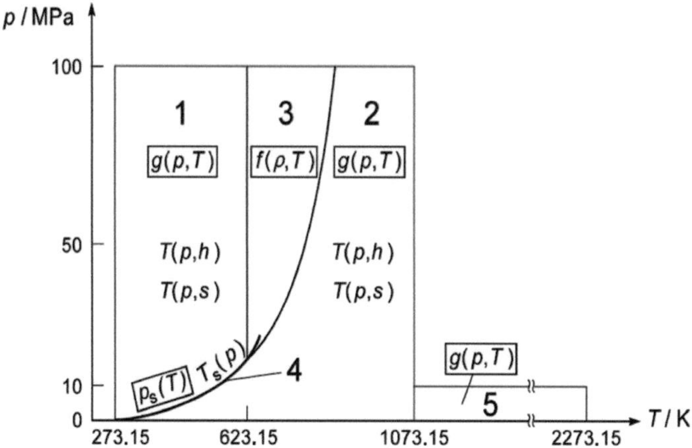

Figure 7. Distribution of thermodynamic property regions for modeling equations by IAPWS [9].

2.3. Drum-evaporator circuit

The evaporator consists of the thermal furnace system that includes drum tank, downcomer tubes, and riser tubes. The fluid circulation can be natural, assisted, or forced. **Figure 8** shows an evaporator thermal circuit that operates with natural water/steam circulation.

The numerical modeling of both control volumes, C.V.1 and C.V.2 shown in **Figure 8**, uses the proposed equations by Vega-Fonseca [16] and Dieck [6, 7, 17, 18], where the following assumptions are made:

- The mass flow rate that enters the downcomers (m_{dc}) equals to the mass flow rate received by the drum tank through the feedwater (m_{ec}).
- The water/steam flow circulation thru the risers and downcomers is constant.
- The liquid water at the drum tank is in saturation.
- The drum is a perfect cylinder.
- The feedwater flow to the drum coming from the economizer is at saturated liquid-water conditions.

The liquid level at the drum is obtained as follows:

$$\frac{dy}{dt} = \frac{\dot{m}_s\left[\frac{A_4}{A_2} - h_v\right] - \dot{m}_{ec}\left[\frac{A_4}{A_2} - h_{ec}\right] + \dot{Q}_r}{A_3 A_0 - \frac{A_1 A_4 A_0}{A_2}} \tag{17}$$

The drum pressure is obtained as follows:

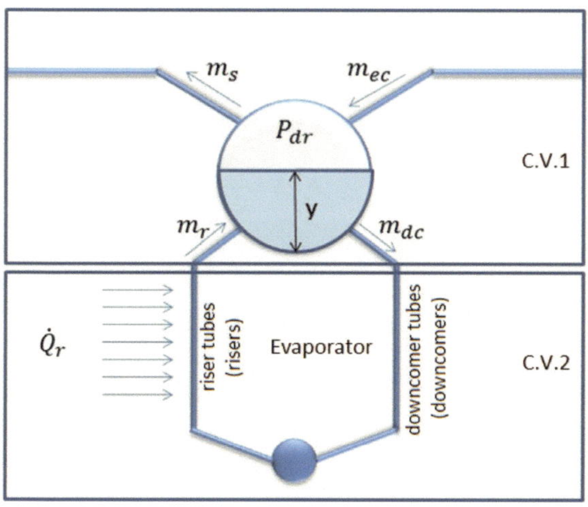

Figure 8. Typical evaporation circuit.

$$\frac{dP}{dt} = \frac{\dot{m}_s\left[\frac{A_3}{A_1} - h_v\right] - \dot{m}_{ec}\left[\frac{A_3}{A_1} - h_{ec}\right] + \dot{Q}_r}{A_4 - \frac{A_3 A_2}{A_1}} \tag{18}$$

The previous equations are complemented using the following Energy balance from the hot flue gases to the water steam as shown in **Figure 9**.

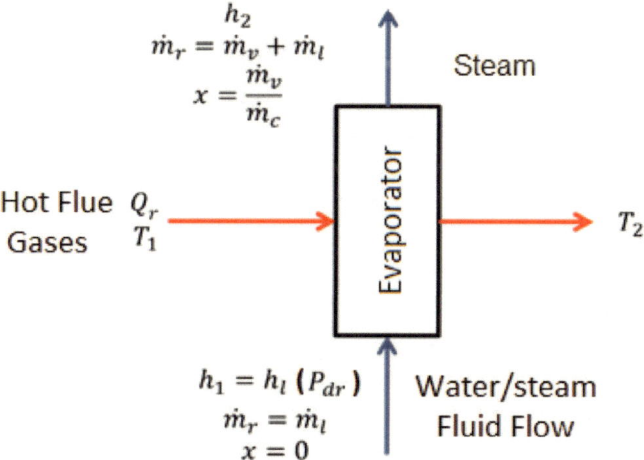

Figure 9. Energy balance at the evaporator.

$$x = \frac{\dot{m}_v}{\dot{m}_r} \tag{19}$$

$$h_1 = h_l(P_{dr}) \tag{20}$$

$$h_{lv} = h_v(P_{dr}) - h_l(P_{dr}) \tag{21}$$

$$h_2 = x h_{lv} + h_1 \tag{22}$$

$$\dot{Q}_r = \dot{m}_r(h_2 - h_1) \tag{23}$$

To obtain the combustion gas temperature at the evaporator exit, the following equation can be used:

$$\dot{Q}_r = \dot{m}_g C_{p_g}(T_2 - T_1) \tag{24}$$

Eqs. (15) and (16) describe the behavior of the drum-evaporator system in terms of the absorbed heat by the evaporator, the drum feedwater flow, and the vapor leaving the drum to the superheated system.

2.4. Shrink and swell model

In some steam generators, changes in temperature and pressure in the evaporator system produces an unbalance condition that generates a reverse effect in the drum level when increasing load conditions [7]. This phenomenon is called shrink and swell due to the vapor bubbles generated in the drum tank that generates the rise and drop of the drum level value. To model this effect, a first order transfer function term equation is proposed as follows:

$$\Delta h = \frac{K(W_{fe} - W_{sh})}{\frac{s}{\tau} + 1} \tag{25}$$

where Δh is the drum level adjustment, τ is the bubble transit time to the drum liquid surface, W_{fe} is the feed-water flow, W_{sh} is the steam flow output to the high temperature exchangers such as the superheater, s is the complex frequency variable (s = jω), and K is a constant of the model in sec/Kg. This equation assumes that the bubbles are lumped into a volume section of the drum cylinder and Eq. (27) describes a first order behavior in transporting this volume to the very top of the liquid surface.

2.5. Control system model

The predicted performance of the HRSG expects the use of a three element drum level control system in the evaporator. This will allow a smooth control in the drum tank dynamic behavior. The configuration is based upon three process variables that are measured during the HRSG operation: output steam flow, drum liquid level and feedwater flow. The control system model assumes the use of PID controllers for the three element control system. Other possibilities exist and can be substituted by the PID algorithms.

http://dx.doi.org/10.5772/intechopen.79410

The standard PID model is as follows:

$$G_c = k_p\left(E_t + \frac{1}{T_i}\int_0^t E_t dt + T_d\frac{dE_t}{dt}\right) \tag{26}$$

$$G_c = k_p\left(E_t + \frac{1}{T_i}\int_0^t E_t dt + T_d\frac{dE_t}{dt}\right)$$

where the discrete formulation is:

$$\Delta G_c = k_p\left[E_t - E_{t-\Delta t} + \frac{\Delta t}{2T_i}(E_t + E_{t-\Delta t}) + \frac{T_d}{\Delta t}(E_t - 2E_{t-\Delta t} + E_{t-2\Delta t})\right] \tag{27}$$

$$\Delta G_c = k_p\left[E_t - E_{t-\Delta t} + \frac{\Delta t}{2T_i}(E_t + E_{t-\Delta t}) + \frac{T_d}{\Delta t}(E_t - 2E_{t-\Delta t} + E_{t-2\Delta t})\right]$$

The first PID controller sets the demand for drum level that is compensated by the feedforward signal from the steam flow as shown in **Figure 10**. The compensated demand signal for drum level is compared to the measured feedwater flow signal to obtain the error signal that feeds the second PID controller that activates the feedwater valve actuator. Therefore, the use of three process signals: drum level, steam flow, and feedwater flow in the HRSG decreases the expansion and contraction behavior in the drum liquid due to sudden changes in steam load. Summarizing the drum level control includes the first PID controller, which determines the liquid level demands, and the second PID controller, which determines the feedwater to the drum tank.

The feedwater flow is controlled by modifying the cross sectional area of the valve, which is the percentage of opening. The following equations illustrate this controlling action.

$$E(AP_{wvy}) = y_r - y, \qquad E(AP_{wv\dot{m}}) = \dot{m}_v - \dot{m}_w$$
$$\Delta AP_{wv} = \Delta G\left[E\left(AP_{wvy}\right)\right] + \Delta G\left[E(AP_{wv\dot{m}})\right] \tag{28}$$

$$\Delta AP_{wv} = \Delta G\left[E\left(AP_{wvy}\right)\right] + \Delta G\left[E(AP_{wv\dot{m}})\right]$$

The steam flow, flowing out of the drum tank, is also modifying using the percentage of opening, however, this controller does not follow the liquid level signal, but the drum pressure of the HRSG. **Figure 11** shows how the drum pressure signal, that generates a demand signal, which is feedforwarded by the steam flow, obtains the demand for the vapor actuator valve. The following equations show the controlling action for the actuator of steam valve.

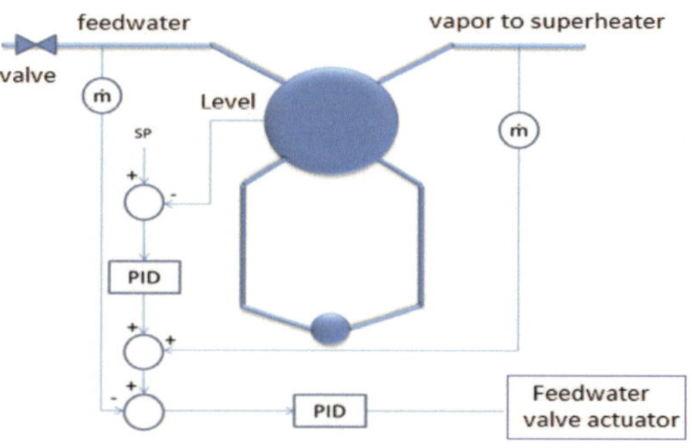

Figure 10. Drum level control system diagram.

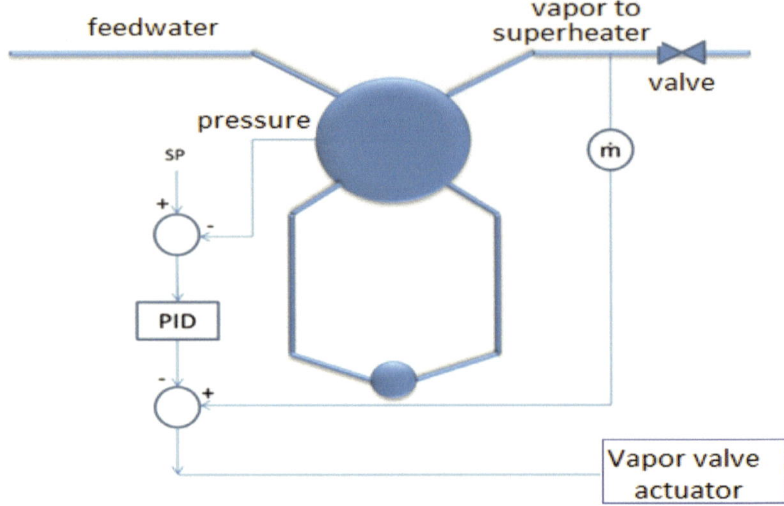

Figure 11. Drum pressure control system diagram.

$$\begin{aligned} E(AP_{sv}) &= P_r - P \\ \Delta AP_{sv} &= \Delta G\left[E(AP_{sv})\right] \end{aligned} \tag{29}$$

Figure 12 shows the steam temperature control system that uses vapor attemperation to regulate the main steam thermal conditions going to the superheater system. The system compares the steam temperature at the superheater 2 outlet with the set point to generate the error. Then the PID controller generates the demand signal to open or close the spray valve, which brings water/vapor at lower temperature than the superheat leaving the drum.

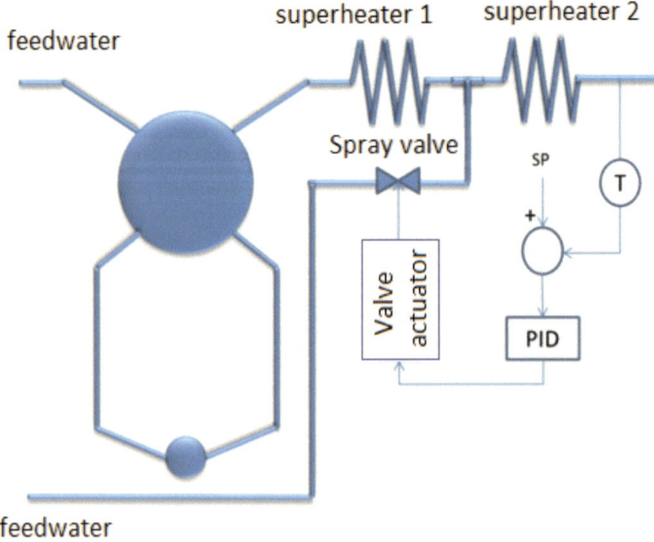

Figure 12. Steam temperature using feedwater attemperation. Control system diagram.

3. Simulator development

Once the equations have been derived, a computer simulation model is developed to initiate the test of the steam generation system predicted performance both, in steady state and dynamic conditions. One of the objectives is to validate a modular simulation feature that permits a fully integration of blocks when additional components are added to the system. The simulation tool would be useful to provide predicted performance behaviors for a wide variety of system configurations based in elementary modules such as preheaters, economizers, evaporators, superheaters, and reheaters. **Figure 13** describes the general operation of a typical computer simulation program where the main computing blocks and variables are described. Further details on the simulation blocks and programs can be found in Ref. [16].

3.1. Case study 1: Modeling and simulation of an industrial boiler

An industrial boiler was modeled and simulated having a traditional PID control strategy. The boiler under test was a VU − 60 Industrial system that produces 180,000 pounds of steam per hour [7]. The mathematical model of the plant was a scaled version model of the one obtained for a thermoelectric unit [6]. The model represented only the behavior of the drum-evaporator system having a combustion process with a simplified control system and a three element boiler feed-water controller. The simulations were performed using the SIMULINK® shell running under the MATLAB® platform.

The computational model obtained is compared with the measurements from the real boiler at steady state as well as during transient conditions. In steady state, four steam loads were studied and they are shown in **Tables 2–5**. In all cases, a small steady state error is observed

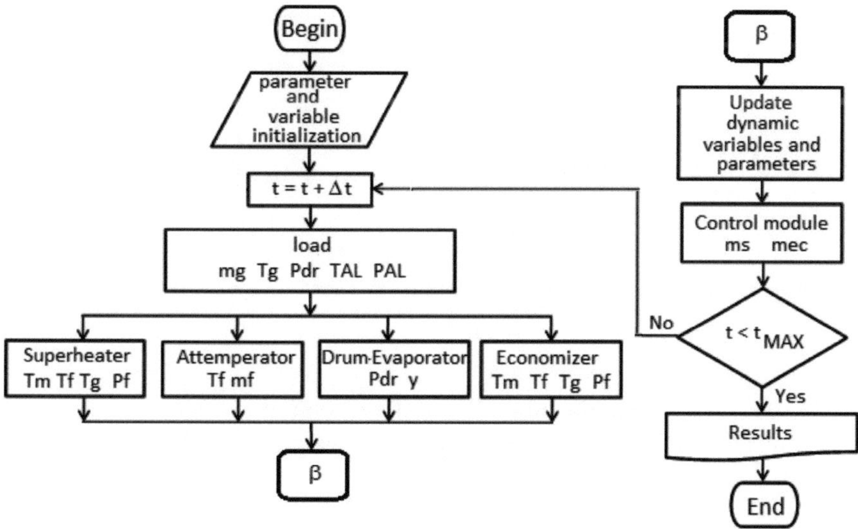

Figure 13. Computer simulation flow diagram.

@56e3 lb/h	Real	Simulated	Error
Steam flow (lb/h)	56.25e+3	56.25e+3	0.00%
Feed-water flow (lb/h)	56.25e+3	56.25e+3	0.00%
Gas flow (lb/h)	3.09e+3	3.18e+3	2.72%
Drum water level (in)	21.28e+0	21.28e+0	0.00%
Drum pressure (psia)	453.84e+0	453.84e+0	0.00%

Table 2. Measurement vs. simulation comparison for a load of 56 × 10^3 lb/h.

@65 e+3 lb/h	Real	Simulated	Error
Steam flow (lb/h)	65.73e+3	65.73e+3	0.00%
Feed-water flow (lb/h)	65.90e+3	65.73e+3	-0.26%
Gas flor (lb/h)	3.77e+3	3.71e+3	-1.55%
Drum water level (in)	25.93e+0	25.93e+0	0.00%
Drum pressure (psia)	445.44e+0	445.44e+0	0.00%

Table 3. Measurement vs. simulation comparison for a load of 65 × 10^3 lb/h.

@135e3 lb/h	Real	Simulated	Error
Steam flow (lb/h)	135.36e+3	135.36e+3	0.00%
Feed-water flow (lb/h)	141.88e+3	135.36e+3	-4.60%
Gas flow (lb/h)	8.04e+3	7.65e+3	-4.77%
Drum water level (in)	25.84e+0	25.84e+0	0.00%
Drum pressure (psia)	474.63e+0	474.63e+0	0.00%

Table 4. Measurement vs. simulation comparison for a load of 135 × 10^3 lb/h.

for the feed-water flow. This error might be produced by a purge located before the sensor position. This way the flow will always be higher in the simulation values.

The simulation of the transient behavior was performed using a load ramp of 1.9% per minute. The results for the critical variables are shown in **Figures 14** and **15**. The error in the feed-water flow is due to a non-minimal phase effect that was not replicated exactly in the model simulation.

@170e3 lb/h	Real	Simulated	Error
Steam flow (lb/h)	170.74E+3	170.74E+3	0.00%
Feed-water flow (lb/h)	175.40E+3	170.74E+3	-2.66%
Gas flow(lb/h)	9.87E+3	9.67E+3	-2.02%
Nivel Agua Domo(in)	25.73E+0	25.73E+0	0.00%
Drum pressure (psia)	502.17E+0	502.17E+0	0.00%

Table 5. Measurement vs. simulation comparison for a load of 170×10^3 lb/h.

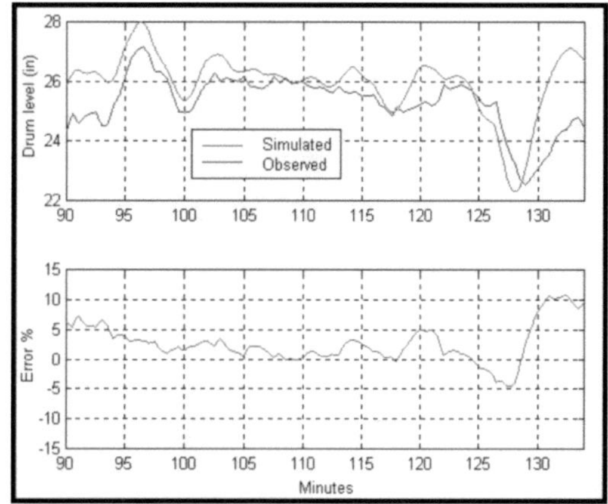

Figure 14. Drum level behavior and error comparing simulation and measurements.

3.2. Case study 2: Modeling and simulation of HRSG

This case shows a heat recovery steam generator (HRSG) operating at different ramping conditions and then settling a steady state operating. The modular simulation methodology permits a full integration of blocks when additional components are added to the system. The simulation tool provides predicted performance behaviors for a wide variety of HRSG configurations based in elementary modules such as preheaters, economizers, evaporators, superheaters, and reheaters. Further details on the simulation blocks and programs can be found in Ref. [16]. **Tables 6** and **7** shows the dimensions and geometries of the system.

The case in point describes the behavior of a load rejection from 100–75% in the turbine gas capacity, by making reductions in the amount of combustion gases as well as in their

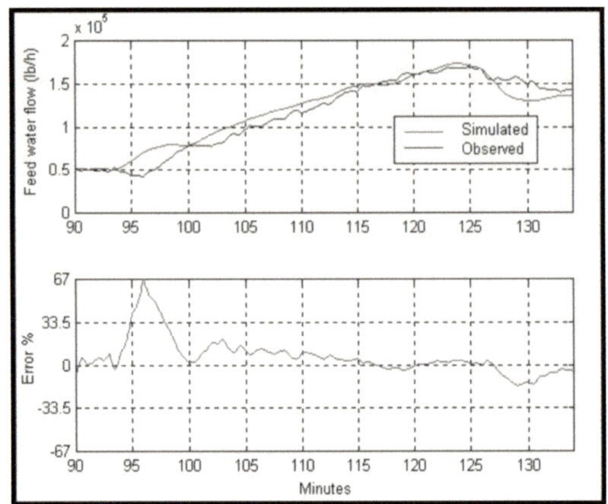

Figure 15. Feedwater flow behavior and error comparing simulation and measurements.

Drum Tank		
Ld	Drum Lenght [m]	10.973
R	Drum Radius [m]	0.991
Y	Drum Liquid Level [m]	50%

Table 6. Geometric configuration of the drum tank.

Geometry		SCAP1	SCAP2	SCAP3	ECAP1	ECAP2
Pl	Longitudinal step [m]	0.117475	0.117475	0.117475	0.092075	0.092075
Pt	Transversal step [m]	0.088011	0.088011	0.088011	0.088011	0.088011
OD	External diameter [m]	0.0381	0.0381	0.0381	0.0381	0.0381
THI	Tube thikness [m]	0.004191	0.003429	0.002667	0.002667	0.002667
Nt	Number of tubes per bed	64	64	64	64	64
Rfo	External waste factor [m^2-K/W]	0.000172	0.000172	0.000172	0.000172	0.000172
Lx	Tube lenght in X {m]	14.249	14.249	14.249	14.249	14.249
NR	Number of tube beds	2	2	2	7	7
la	Fin lenght [m]	0.009525	0.015875	0.015875	0.015875	0.015875
ta	Fin thickness [m]	0.000991	0.000991	0.000991	0.000991	0.000991
na	Number of fins per meter	118.1	226.4	226.4	259.8	258.9
Ws	Fin width [m]	0.003988	0.003988	0.003988	0.003988	0.003988
Rug	Absolute internal tube roughness [m]	0.000045	0.000045	0.000045	0.000045	0.000045

Table 7. Geometric configuration of the heat exchanger elements in the HRSG system.

temperatures. **Table 8** shows the how the variables change in the 900 seconds test. The control system generates corrective actions in order to sustain the liquid level and drum fluid pressure at the predicted performance. **Table 9** compares the simulated experiment results with the

100 to 75% ramping	Difference between loads	Rate of change per second
✱T_g (gas temp, °C)	-60	-0.067
✱m_g (gas mass flow, Kg/s)	-13.29	-0.015
✱T_f (steam temp, °C)	-9.5	-0.011
✱P_f (steam pressure, Bars)	-25.03	-0.028
✱P_{dr} (drum steam pressure, Bars)	-24.13	-0.027

Table 8. Variations of temperature, mass flow and pressures for 100–75% ramp.

predicted performance for the superheater systems. **Table 10** compares the simulated experiment results with the predicted performance for the evaporator and economizer systems.

Table 9 shows a 1.56% difference between the simulated steam flow at superheater 1 from the steady state predicted performance at 100% load. This result is due to a slight overestimation of the steam temperature at superheater 3 that induces the control system to inject spray water to regulate the steam temperature according to the reference value. **Table 10** shows also an overestimation of feedwater temperature at economizer 2. This temperature difference is 3.3% higher than the predicted performance for the HRSG system. However, those differences are well within the desired specifications of similar computer simulation systems. At the 75% load

		100% Load			75% Load		
		SIM	PERFORMANCE	ERROR	SIM	PERFORMANCE	ERROR
Hot Flue Gas Flow [Kg/s]		1213485.00	1213485.00	0.00%	1083578.00	1083578.00	0.00%
SUPERHEATER AP 1		SIM	PERFORMANCE	ERROR	SIM	PERFORMANCE	ERROR
STEAM FLOW [Kg/s]		203931.43	200800.00	-1.56%	149449.00	149449.00	0.00%
INLET	GAS TEMP [°C]	622.20	622.20	0.00%	562.20	562.20	0.00%
	FLUID TEMP [°C]	459.40	458.90	-0.11%	466.59	458.30	-1.81%
	FLUIDPRESSURE[bar	92.89	92.87	-0.02%	69.45	69.43	-0.03%
OUTLET	GAS TEMP [°C]	605.18	605.60	0.07%	552.56	552.20	-0.07%
	FLUID TEMP [°C]	501.74	503.30	0.31%	497.07	492.80	-0.87%
	FLUIDPRESSURE[bar	89.74	89.91	0.19%	67.12	67.22	0.14%
SUPERHEATER AP 2		SIM	PERFORMANCE	ERROR	SIM	PERFORMANCE	ERROR
STEAM FLOW [Kg/s]		203931.43	200703.00	-1.61%	149449.00	149449.00	0.00%
INLET	GAS TEMP [°C]	605.18	605.07	-0.02%	552.56	552.20	-0.07%
	FLUID TEMP [°C]	362.63	371.10	2.28%	384.14	376.70	-1.97%
	FLUIDPRESSURE[bar	94.92	94.46	-0.49%	71.02	70.67	-0.50%
OUTLET	GAS TEMP [°C]	560.45	569.40	1.57%	524.80	526.10	0.25%
	FLUID TEMP [°C]	459.40	459.40	0.00%	466.59	458.30	-1.81%
	FLUIDPRESSURE[bar	92.89	93.56	0.72%	69.45	69.91	0.66%
SUPERHEATER AP 3		SIM	PERFORMANCE	ERROR	SIM	PERFORMANCE	ERROR
STEAM FLOW [Kg/s]		197303.00	197303.00	0.00%	149449.00	149449.00	0.00%
INLET	GAS TEMP [°C]	560.45	560.45	0.00%	524.80	526.10	0.25%
	FLUID TEMP [°C]	308.11	308.30	0.06%	287.72	288.30	0.20%
	FLUIDPRESSURE[bar	96.13	95.77	-0.37%	71.98	71.71	-0.38%
OUTLET	GAS TEMP [°C]	509.63	509.63	0.00%	481.11	487.80	1.37%
	FLUID TEMP [°C]	389.58	382.80	-1.77%	384.13	376.70	-1.97%
	FLUIDPRESSURE[bar	94.92	95.15	0.24%	71.02	71.22	0.28%

Components: Superheaters AP-1, AP-2 and AP-3

Table 9. Comparison between initial and final loads for a download change from 100–75%.

		100% Load			75% Load		
EVAPORATOR		SIM	PERFORMANCE	ERROR	SIM	PERFORMANCE	ERROR
STEAM FLOW [Kg/s]		197303.00	197303.00	0.00%	149449.00	149449.00	0.00%
INLET	GAS TEMP [°C]	509.63	524.40	2.82%	481.11	487.80	1.37%
	FLUID TEMP [°C]	308.11	300.60	-2.50%	287.72	286.10	-0.57%
	FLUIDPRESSURE[bar	96.13	96.11	-0.02%	71.98	71.98	0.00%
OUTLET	GAS TEMP [°C]	325.49	328.30	0.86%	306.18	305.00	-0.39%
	FLUID TEMP [°C]	308.11	308.90	0.26%	287.72	288.90	0.41%
	FLUIDPRESSURE[bar	96.13	96.11	-0.02%	71.98	71.98	0.00%
ECONOMIZER AP 1		SIM	PERFORMANCE	ERROR	SIM	PERFORMANCE	ERROR
STEAM FLOW [Kg/s]		197308.000	197308.000	0.00%	149449.000	149449.000	0.00%
INLET	GAS TEMP [°C]	323.99	323.90	-0.03%	301.18	300.00	-0.39%
	FLUID TEMP [°C]	267.95	259.40	-3.30%	258.74	259.40	0.25%
	FLUIDPRESSURE[bar	97.28	96.94	-0.35%	72.55	72.46	-0.12%
OUTLET	GAS TEMP [°C]	292.89	292.20	-0.24%	282.95	275.00	-2.89%
	FLUID TEMP [°C]	307.85	300.60	-2.41%	288.08	286.10	-0.69%
	FLUIDPRESSURE[bar	96.73	96.11	-0.65%	72.24	71.98	-0.36%
ECONOMIZER AP 2		SIM	PERFORMANCE	ERROR	SIM	PERFORMANCE	ERROR
STEAM FLOW [Kg/s]		197303.00	197303.00	0.00%	124501.00	124502.00	0.00%
INLET	GAS TEMP [°C]	292.89	292.20	-0.24%	282.95	275.00	-2.89%
	FLUID TEMP [°C]	185.60	185.60	0.00%	176.10	176.10	0.00%
	FLUIDPRESSURE[bar	97.77	97.77	0.00%	72.74	72.74	0.00%
OUTLET	GAS TEMP [°C]	237.63	242.20	1.89%	244.58	235.00	-4.08%
	FLUID TEMP [°C]	267.95	259.40	-3.30%	258.74	259.40	0.25%
	FLUIDPRESSURE[bar	97.28	96.94	-0.35%	72.55	72.46	-0.12%

Components: Evaporator, Economizer AP-1 and Economizer AP-

Table 10. Comparison between initial and final loads for a download change from 100 to 75%.

a hot flue gases temperature error of 4.07% above the predicted performance is obtained from the computer simulation.

4. Conclusions

This chapter presents a methodology of a modeling and simulation of the steam generation process conceived as a development tool that permits the evaluation of different operating conditions of Industrial Boiler and HRSG systems. The objective is to support critical engineering decisions with respect to design, fault evaluation, and integrated analysis. Also, the simulation system allows the development of simulation exercises about interest scenarios to determine important multivariable cause-effects in both, industrial boilers and HRSG systems, without exposing the equipment to harmful and costly operative tests.

Two case studies are shown with validation tables both, in steady state and dynamic conditions. Even though the mathematical models are simplified, the results provide enough precision to study very complex dynamical behavior of this multivariable thermal process. Results show a difference of less than 5% with respect to the manufacturer's predicted performances in critical values of drum pressure, steam flow, steam temperatures, and hot flue gases flow. The numerical stability of the simulation behaves well due to the robustness of the discretization methodology and numerical methods used in the simulation model. The simulation model generates accumulated discrepancies and errors between 2 and 5% in temperature errors for the heat exchanger models such as economizers and superheaters. The drum pressure follows the main steam demand as expected and the hot flue gases have a slight overshoot when the ramp ends at full nominal load. The controller showed a good performance maintaining the drum liquid level steady during all simulation exercises. Finally, the modular approach used can be expanded to include different geometric configurations and operating conditions, as well as different tuning alternatives for the control system [19–22].

Glossary

A	area (m^2)
c_p	specific heat at constant pressure (J/kg K)
c_v	specific heat at constant volume (J/kg K)
D	diameter (m)
E	error as a function of time
G	transfer function
g	gravity (m/s^2)
HRSG	heat recovery steam generator
h	entalpy (J/kg) or heat transfer coefficient (W/m^2K)
k_p	proportional gain
L	length (m)
M	mass (kg)
$\dot{m}$	mass flow rate (kg/s)
N_R	number of tube beds (or levels)
N_T	number of tubes per bed
P	pressure (bar)
P_l	longitudinal step (m)
P_t	transversal step (m)
PM	molecular weight (kg/moles)
P_r	Prandtl number
$\dot{Q}$	heat transfer rate (W)
r	radius (m)
Re	Reynolds number
t	time (s)

T	temperature (K)
T_i	integral time constant (s)
T_d	derivative time constant (s)
u	specific internal energy (J/kg)
V	velocity (m/s) or volume (m^3)
v	specific volume (m^3/kg)
x	coordinate x or vapor quality
Y	volumetric fraction
y	coordinate y or level (m)
f_d	friction coefficient
ε	roughness (m)
ξ	flow resistance coefficient
Υ	specific heat ratio
η	efficiency
D	change
λ	thermal conductivity (W/m K)
ρ	density (kg/m^3)
m	dynamic viscosity (Pa s)
Abbreviations	
EVAP	high pressure evaporator
ECAP	high pressure economizer
TEF	inlet fluid temperature
TSF	outlet fluid temperature
TEG	inlet gas temperature
TSG	outlet gas temperature
SCAP	high pressure superheater
Sub-indices	
c	refers to compound
dc	refers to downcomers
dr	refers to drum tank

ec	refers to economizer
f	refers to internal fluid
fm	refers to the transfer from fluid to metal
g	refers to gas
gm	refers to the transfer from gas to metal
h	refers to hydraulics
I	refers to internal
ll	refers to liquid water
m	refers to metal
mix	refers to a mixture
o	refers to external
r	refers to riser tubes or refers to reference value
s	refers to superheater
v	refers to water vapor
wh	refers to water header
ws	refers to the main steam valve
wv	refers to the feed-water valve

Author details

Graciano Dieck-Assad*, José Luis Vega-Fonseca, Isaías Hernández-Ramírez and Antonio Favela-Contreras

*Address all correspondence to: graciano.dieck.assad@itesm.mx

Mechatronics and Electrical Engineering Department, Tecnológico de Monterrey, Monterrey Campus, Monterrey, México

References

[1] Tomei GL. Steam Its Generation and Use, 42nd ed. Charlotte, North Caroline, U.S.A.: The Babcock & Wilcox Company; 2015

[2] Starr F. Background to the Design of HRSG Systems and Implications for CCGT Plant Cycling. OMNI. 2003;**2**

[3] Stultz SC, Kitto JB, editors. Steam, Its Generation and Use, "Combined Cycles, Waste Heat Recovery and Other Steam Systems". 40th ed. Barberton OH: Babcock and Wilcox Co.; 1992. 31.1–31.13

[4] Mansour FM. Combined Cycle Dynamics. IMechE Proc. Instn. Mech. Engrs., Vol. 217 Part A: J. Power and Energy; 2003

[5] Dumont M-N. Mathematical modelling and design of advanced once-through heat recovery steam generator. Computers and Chemical Engineering, Elsevier. 2004;**28**(651):660

[6] Dieck-Assad G. Development of a state boiler model for process optimization. Simulation. 1990;**55**:201-213

[7] Dieck-Assad G. Modeling and simulation of a fuzzy supervisory controller for an industrial boiler. Simulation. 2006;**82**:841-850

[8] Nakamura S. Metodos numericos aplicados con software. Mexico: Pearson; 1992

[9] Zukauskas A. Heat Transfer from Tubes in Cross Flow. New York: Wiley Interscience; 1987

[10] International Association for the Properties of Water and Steam. IAPWS Industrial Formulation 1997 for the Thermodynamic Properties of Water and Steam

[11] Yaws, C. Yaws' 2003. Handbook of Thermodynamic and Physical Properties of Chemical Compounds. s.l.: Knovel

[12] American Society of Mechanical Engineers. 2001 ASME Boiler and Pressure Vessel Code, Section II–Materials, Subpart 2

[13] Crane Co. Flow of fluids through valves, fittings and pipe. Technical paper No. 410; 2009

[14] Incropera F. Fundamentals of Heat and Mass Transfer. 6th ed. USA: Wiley; 2007

[15] Holman JP. Heat Transfer. 6th ed. USA: McGraw-Hill; 1986

[16] Vega-Fonseca JL. Development of a simulator to study transients in Heat Recovery Steam Generator HRSG processes. Master's Thesis. Tecnológico de Monterrey, Monterrey Campus, México; 2012

[17] Dieck-Assad G. Midium Scale Modeling and Controller Optimization of a Boiler Turbine System. Phd dissertation. University of Texas at Austin, Austin, Texas, USA; 1984

[18] Dieck Assad G. Controllability and Optimization of Main Steam Temperature in Boilers with Burner Tilting, IEEE Mexicon. Guadalajara, Jalisco, Mexico; 1992

[19] Rovira V. A model to predict the behavior at part load operation of once-through heat recovery steam generators working with water at supercritical pressure. Applied Thermal Engineering. 2010;**30**:1652-1658

[20] Lee K. Analysis of thermal stress evolution in the steam drum during start-up of a heat recovery steam generator. International Journal of Energy Research. 2000;**24**(137):149

[21] Astrom KJL. Drum boiler dynamics. Automatica. 2000;**36**:363-378

[22] ALSTOM Clean Combustion Technologies. A Reference Book on Steam Generation and Emission Controls. 5th ed; 2010

Chapter 3

Agent-Based Modeling and Simulation of Biological Systems

Şebnem Bora and Sevcan Emek

Additional information is available at the end of the chapter

http://dx.doi.org/10.5772/intechopen.80070

Abstract

Agent-based modeling and simulation is a powerful technique in simulating and exploring phenomena that includes a large set of active components represented by agents. The agents are actors operating in a real system, influencing the simulated environment and influenced by the simulated environment. The agents are included in the simulation model as model components performing actions autonomously and interacting with other agents and the simulated environment to represent behaviors in the real system. In this chapter, we describe how to develop an agent-based model and simulation for biological systems in Repast Simphony platform, which is a Java-based modeling system. Repast Simphony helps developers to create a scenario tree including displays of agents, grid and continuous space, data sets, data loaders, histogram, and time charts. At the end of this chapter, we present case studies developed by our research group with references to demonstrate local behavior of biological system.

Keywords: agent, agent-based modeling and simulation, biological systems, Repast Simphony

1. Introduction

In recent years, agent-based applications have been developed inspired by natural systems. The natural systems have a dynamic structure defined by a complex, distributed, open, heterogeneous, and large-scale systems. Therefore, it is too hard to model these systems in the artificial world. Agent-based modeling and simulation (ABMS) technique has advantage in explanation of the dynamics of the behavior in the complex systems including biological, physical, and social systems. ABMS which is used in the solution or modeling of a problem

in the literature seems to be inspired by living systems. Living systems offer an organization and operation at different levels ranging from the genetic to the social experience. The most common applications that can be shown in living systems are biological systems including human physiology which examine major systems such as cardiovascular system, immune system, nervous system, endocrine system, etc., and predator-prey relationship in the ecosystem, birds and fish flocks, organisms that live in colonies such as foraging ants, bees, wasps, and termites, and etc. [1].

ABMS allows the researchers an experimental experience to create, analyze, and explicate the relationship between the artificial and the real world. In comparison with other modeling approach based on mathematical and numerical analysis, control theory, biomechanical techniques, etc., ABMS is referred to as "individual-based model" [2]. Individual is called agent which has a set of attributes and autonomous behavior. Agents are situated in some set of spaces and time. Agents interact with other agents in the simulation environment. The simulation environment includes agents that perform their actions and achieve their goals.

In this chapter, we will focus on the use of computer simulation for building the agent-based models in biological systems. This chapter intends to provide brief descriptions of the agent-based models that illustrate how to build and implement case studies, which reflect the relationship in the real world.

This chapter is organized as follows: Section 2 gives a brief overview of ABMS; Section 3 presents the description of Repast Simphony toolkit which has ability to display and schedule in real time; Section 4 provides implementation of case studies involving different scenarios to better understand ABMS phenomena; and Section 5 concludes with a brief summary of this chapter.

2. Agent-based modeling and simulation

Agent-based modeling and simulation (ABMS) can be defined in very diverse disciplines like artificial intelligence, complexity science, game theory, etc. [3, 4]. ABMS provides a suitable simulation modeling technique for the analysis of complex systems and emergent phenomena in biological systems, social sciences, economy, management systems, etc. [5, 6]. ABMS is a computational model implemented as computer simulation in which there are individual entities and their behaviors and interactions. It focuses on rules and interaction among the individuals or components of the real system. In the ABMS, the systems are characterized by the autonomous and independent entities known as agents performing some kind of behaviors (action and interactions) in the simulation environment [7]. In the literature, it is possible to see many examples of agent-based modeling in the different fields including traffic control, biomedical research, ecology, energy analysis, etc. [4].

ABMS has advantage of creating a model compared to traditional approaches. No any set of formulas or mathematical equations are needed to build an agent-based model. ABMS focuses on the rules that will determine the behaviors of agents [8]. In order to develop an agent-based model, firstly, it must be understood how to design and implement the model. In other words, the scenario of a real system must determine the limitations of the model. Some questions must be answered to initialize the model design, like what the agents should be in the model, what the agents' environment is, how to interact with each other and environment, how to define the rules determined the behaviors of agents, what are roles of the agents in the model, etc. [9].

There are some simulation software toolkits to perform ABMS [10]. Toolkits can facilitate to manage the simulation process. One of the most popular toolkits in the literature is Repast Simphony supported by libraries of predefined methods and functions [11, 12].

3. Repast Simphony

Repast (Recursive Porous Agent Simulation Toolkit) Simphony is an agent-based modeling and simulation framework based on the object-oriented programming using Java language. It is free and open source so that it offers the users the widespread use of the agent development environments. Repast Simphony uses Eclipse-integrated development environment (IDE) for developing computer code [13]. Repast Simphony tool offers researchers a flexible way to write models including graphical user interface, toolbar to control the simulation processes (start, step, pause, stop, exit, etc.), displaying agents and their environment, monitoring the output data (time chart, histogram bar), scheduling of simulations, parameter management, data sets, data loaders, etc. Repast Simphony is the most suitable simulation framework for agent-based model development. Classes of agents and their interactions are displayed in Repast Simphony. The output data are graphically presented in time charts and/or histogram bar. Repast Simphony allows the users to record inbuilt data to txt files and displays as movies or images. Also, the users obtain the snapshots of graphics and/or display. Repast Simphony has advantage to display, schedule, analyze, update, or manipulate a running simulation in real time.

After downloading the latest version on Repast Simphony from its web page, creating a new Repast Simphony project is very easy. The first step is to run Eclipse IDE. After the new Repast Simphony Project, which includes a source directory, and default package is created, the scenario directory structure is prepared by creating agent classes.

To build an agent-based model, it is necessary to create classes. More agent classes can be created according to the scenario of the model. The classes include any number of methods to describe the attributes and roles of agents. Setup or step methods are called for each iteration of the simulation. In the each iteration of the simulation, the simulation runtime is described with time steps or tick counts. During the simulation runtime, the agents perform their actions. The get and set methods, which describe agents' attributes, may update the value returned or stored in each tick count. The agents may continue or update their actions according to the results of the previous action they performed.

Agents are situated in continuous space and/or grid in the simulation environment which provides a context for interaction and communication of agents. Agents may be distributed to the environment randomly or with some rules. They may have the energy to make them survive. If the agent's energy is exhausted, the agent may die. If the agent's energy reaches the reproduction threshold, it may reproduce. In the simulation environment, there are heterogeneous agents which have different types. For example, an agent may represent the animal, while the other may represent the human. A style class in two-dimensional (2D) or three-dimensional (3D) simulation environment can be created in a way that defines the physical properties of agents such as size, color, and shape. Global parameters associated with agent classes, including initial values of project given by users, may be defined in an xml file.

Repast Simphony provides the users a graphical user interface (GUI). GUI allows the users to manage the simulation processes and to control the parameters. GUI has a user panel that includes run options, parameters, and scenario tree. To form the scenario tree of a project, context builder Java file is defined in data loaders to display agents and the environment on which agents are located. It is possible to observe agents' behavior outputs on the plots and charts. Data sets are created to graphically illustrate time charts defining variables over time. The data set source is determined by pointing out the relevant methods. Histogram bar chart illustrates the distribution of variables.

4. Implementation of the case studies

Agent-based models utilizing Repast Simphony have been developed for a diverse range of scenario including biological systems. In this chapter, three different case studies are presented to better understand ABMS phenomena. These case studies described in subsections are highlighted local behaviors of a real system.

4.1. Sunn pest-wheat

This case study [14] presents the predator prey relationship model in the ecology. In this model, three types of agents are defined as sunn pest, wheat, and parasitoid. The sunn pest called bug agent in the model is both the predator and the prey roles. Wheat called habitat in the model is a cereal plant widely cultivated for food. The sunn pest is fed with wheat grain. The parasitoid is the predator which parasitizes the sunn pest's eggs. We have a grid where the sunn pests are randomly distributed illustrated in **Figure 1**.

The grid includes sunn pest, wheat, and parasitoid. In **Figure 2**, the green color shades indicate the growth of wheat, the red color cells indicate the sunn pest, and the white color cells indicate sunn pests' nymphs. About 7000 sunn pest agents and 1000 parasitoid agents are randomly distributed in the 28,000 grid cells.

In modeling of sunn pest-wheat scenario, agent classes and methods are built according to the definitions in **Tables 1–3**.

The simulation runs during 90th tick counts which is represented in sunn pests' lifecycle (biological stages) and cultivation cycle of wheat. The aim of this case study is to simulate

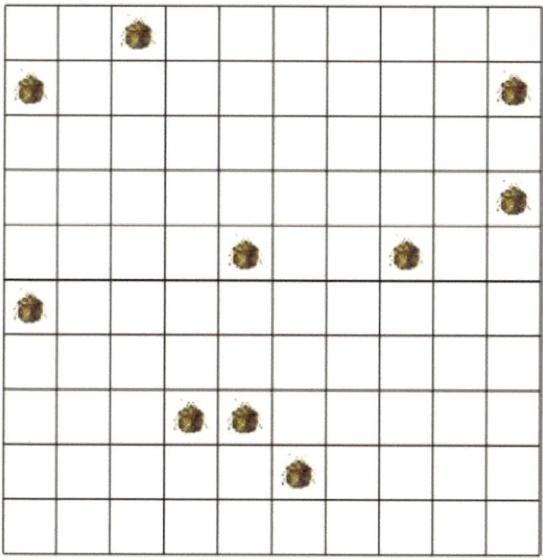

Figure 1. Distribution of the sunn pests on the 10 × 10 grid size.

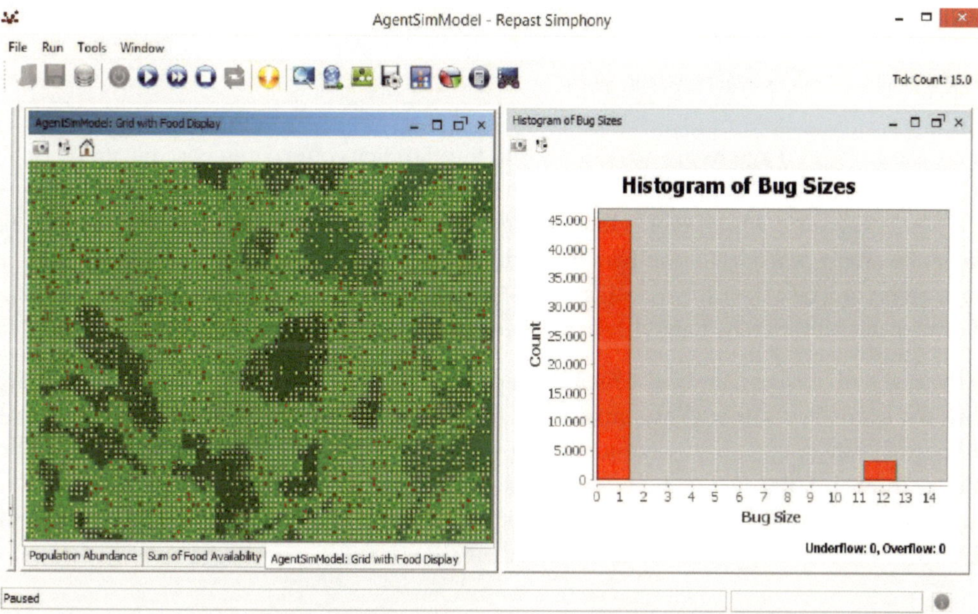

Figure 2. The graphical user interface during the running of the simulation [14].

the chemical and/or biological struggles against sunn pest and obtaining maximum gain to produce the wheat. The parasitoids are used only in biological struggles against sunn pest. In the initial time, all of agents distribute randomly on the grid. If the biological struggle is to be

Roles	**Predator, prey**
Attributes	Size, energy, gender, survival probability, state, generation
Actions	Move, grow, mortality, reproduce, die
Rules	Female and male ratio is 50%.
	Randomly goes to one of the neighbour cells around him and feeds and grows from that cell.
	When the adults come to the field, the simulation starts.
	If the sunn pest is female and its size is more than 12 mm (i.e. the biological state is mature), lay eggs 5 times, leaves a total of 80 to 150 eggs and dies.
	If the sunn pest is a male, it dies in condition that the probability of survival (95%) being smaller than a random number determined.
	Grows 0.3 mm per step in the embryo phase and except this; it grows as much as the amount that it eats.
	If the size of sunn pest is in the range of 0 - 0.8, its biological stage is an "Embryo".
	If the size of sunn pest is in the range of 0.8 - 2.0, its biological stage is a "First nymph".
	If the size of sunn pest is in the range of 2.0 - 3.5, its biological stage is an "Second nymph".
	If the size of sunn pest is in the range of 3.5 - 5.0, its biological stage is a "Third nymph".
	If the size of sunn pest is in the range of 5.0 - 6.0, its biological stage is a "Fourth nymph".
	If the size of sunn pest is in the range of 6.0 - 6.0, its biological stage is a "Fifth nymph".
	If the size of sunn pest is greater than 10.0 mm, its biological stage is in the "Adult".

Table 1. Local knowledge of sunn pest (bug agent).

done, the parasitoid agents are activated. Until the 15th tick count, sunn pest agents act on the grid and fed from the habitat cells. At the 15th tick count, female sunn pests lay eggs (embryos) and die. In **Figure 2**, white color cells on the grid indicate the embryos, and the histogram bar shows the sunn pests' total numbers for each biological stage. Through 90th tick counts, the sunn pests complete their lifecycle against the parasitoid. At the end of the simulation, the sum of food availability on the habitat cells has been observed illustrated in **Figure 3**.

In the result of this case study, the relationship between sunn pest and parasitoid is simulated with the agent-based modeling approach. This case study represents the behavior of a real biological system, even if it is not identified with all the details. In the computer simulation studies, some assumptions can be done, such as in this study, the climate conditions are not included in the simulation. The boundaries of the study must be specified, otherwise undesirable results can be obtained and the system drifts the chaos.

4.2. Bacteria – antibiotic

This work [15] presents bacterial population and resistance to antibiotics. Bacterial population known as bacterial flora are nonharmful microorganisms in the human body that live in the human skin, in the mouth, in the digestive system, etc. There are immune cells that suppress the bacterial flora. Immune cells and bacterial flora should always be balanced in the body. In this model, two types of agents are defined as bacteria and immune system cell. About 4000

Roles	Food value layer
Attributes	production rate, availability value
Actions	grow
Rules	Defined at certain ratio within each cell in the grid.
	Grows certain ratio in each step, and it becomes availability value.
	The sunn pest consumes food as much as its growth rate in the cell where it is located.
	Its color scale changes according to its production rate.

Table 2. Local knowledge of wheat (habitat cell).

Roles	Parasitoid
Attributes	—
Actions	move, hunt, kill
Rules	Randomly distributed in the grid.
	Parasitizes sunn pest's embriyo at the neighbouring cells around and locates in its cell.
	If there is no sunn pest's embriyo in the neighbouring cells, it changes its position and randomly moves to another cell.
	Remains in the grid until the end of the simulation.

Table 3. Local knowledge of parasitoid.

bacterial agents and 100 immune system cell agents are randomly distributed on the 100 × 100 grid cells. The grid represents a human tissue or organ.

Bacteria agents are grouped within themselves depending on the range of disease called virulence factor. The virulence factor is assigned between 1 and 4. In **Figure 4**, the white cells on the grid indicate the bacterial agents which have the virulence factor of 1, the yellow cells on the grid indicate the bacterial agents which have the virulence factor of 2, the red cells on the grid indicate the bacterial agents which have the virulence factor of 3, the purple cells on the grid indicate the bacterial agents which have the virulence factor of 4, and the blue cells on the grid indicate the immune system cell agents which have the virulence factor of 4.

The simulation has three parts: the first one is bacterial competition on flora, the second is antibiotic usage, and the third is antibiotic resistance. According to these parts, the local knowledge of bacterial agents and immune system cell agents is defined in **Table 4**.

In the first part of the simulation, the aim is to balance the population of bacterial agents and immune system cell agents on the grid. Also, bacterial agents compete with their neighbors for space and food resources. A food layer is defined in the simulation environment to live, grow, and reproduce. In the second part of the simulation, antibiotic usage is defined against the bacterial agents. An antibiotic layer is included in the simulation environment. The aim is to help the immune system cell agents and kill the bacterial agents.

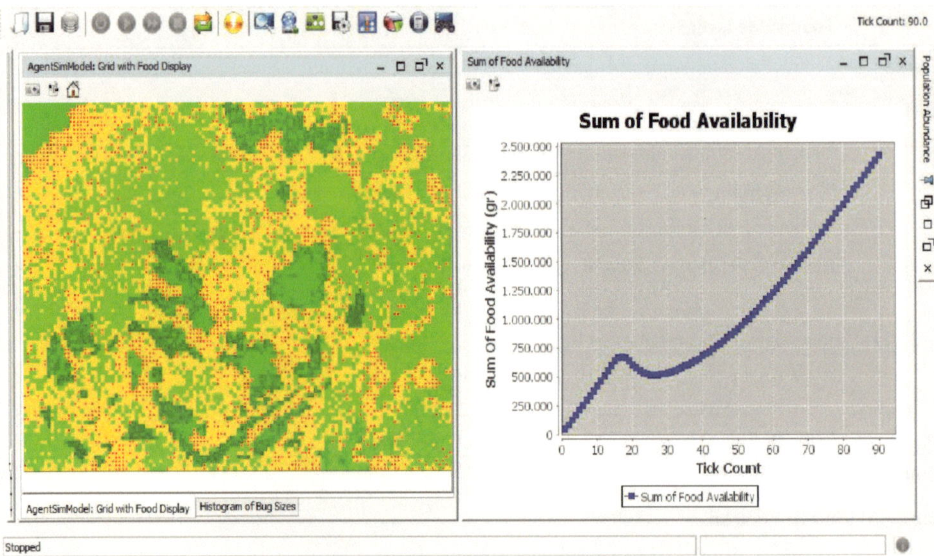

Figure 3. The graphical user interface at the end of simulation [14].

Figure 4. Bacterial agents and immune system cell agents on the grid at the initial time [15].

Figure 5 shows how the antibiotic usage suppresses the bacterial agent population when the immune system cell agents are insufficient. The third part of the simulation presents the relationship between antibiotic-resistant bacterial agents and immune system cell agents. Most of the bacterial agents with virulence factor between 2 and 4 are killed by the antibiotic, whereas rest is killed by immune system cell agents. However, bacterial agents with virulence factor of 1 survive because they are antibiotic-resistant. Bacterial agents with low virulence factor are

	Bacterial agents	Immune system cell agents
Roles	microorganism	microorganism
Attributes	virulance factor, survivalProbability, mutationProbability, size	Id
Actions	move, grow, reproduce	move, send signal, kill, disappear
Rules	Randomly distributed in the grid.	Observes the neighbour 48 cells.
	Divided up into empty cells during the simulation runtime.	If there is a bacteria agent in the neighbour cells, it kills and locates on that cell.
	With a low virulence factor reproduce very rapidly.	If it kills two bacteria, it sends signals to another immune system cell agent and dies.
	With the virulence factor of 1 is resistant to antibiotic which has a concentration value that can kill bacteria in each cell.	If there are more than 40 bacteria agents in the neighbour cells, it sends signals to other immune system cell agents.
		If there are between 2 and 15 bacteria agents in the neighbour cells, it does not see any danger state and disappear.

Table 4. The local knowledge of bacterial agents and immune system cell agents.

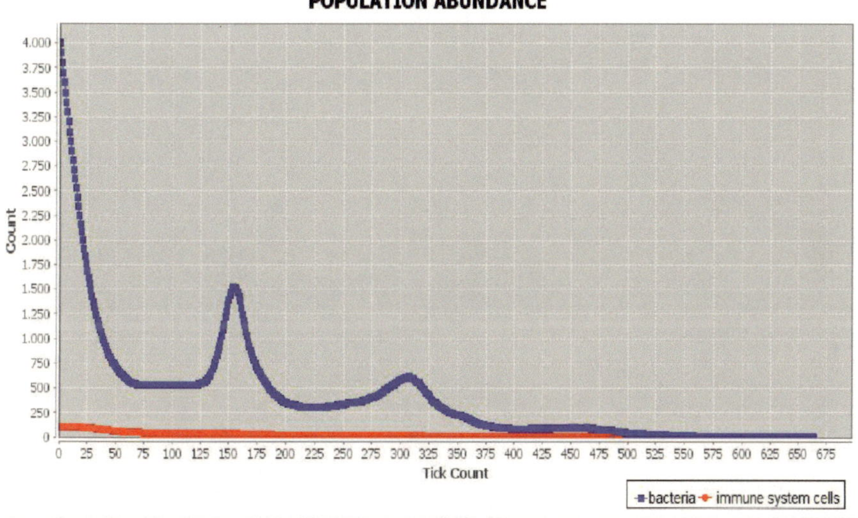

Figure 5. Relationship between bacterial agents and immune system cell agents in the antibiotic usage [15].

divided very rapidly so that the number of immune system cell agents is increased. **Figure 6** shows the struggle between immune system cell agents and bacterial agents on the grid. The grid, which indicates green color in **Figure 6**, represents tissue/organ.

Figure 7 shows, graphically, the populations of immune system cell agents and bacterial agents during the simulation runtime. At the initial time, there are 4000 bacterial agents and

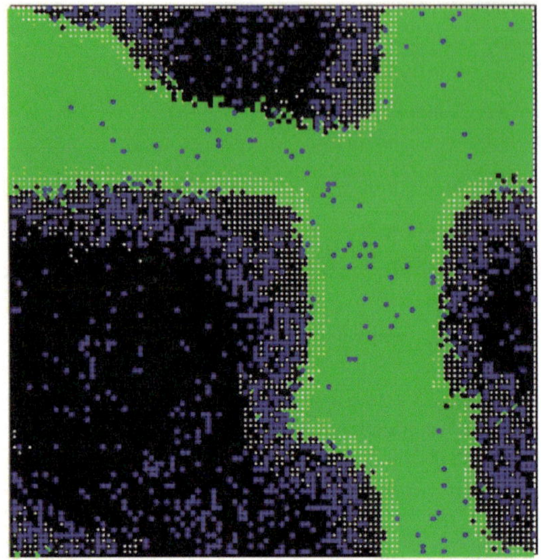

Figure 6. Struggle between immune system cell agents and bacterial agents [15].

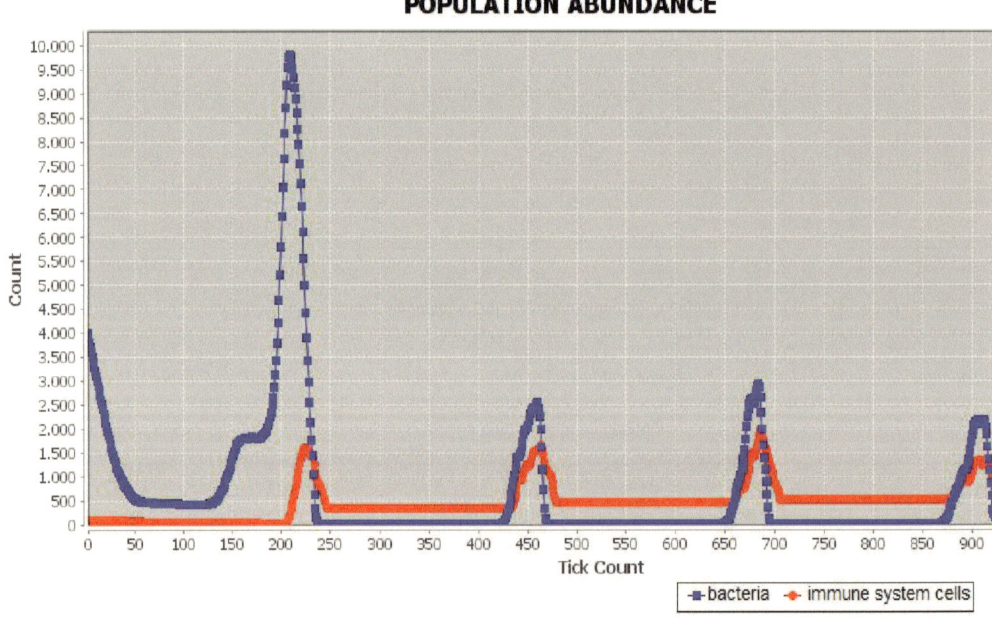

Figure 7. Relationship between bacterial agents and immune system cell agents in the antibiotic usage [15].

100 immune system cell agents on the grid. When simulation starts, immune system cell agents kill some of the bacterial agents. Surviving bacterial agents grow and reproduce. When the population of bacterial agents reaches the maximum value, the population of immune

system cell agents starts to increase. Antibiotic usage helps to reduce the population of bacterial agents because the population of bacterial agents is very large.

This case study provides an introduction to understand the dynamics of microbiological systems that take place in the process of bacterial evolution. During the simulation runtime, it is observed that how the system dynamics can be adaptive to external influences and effect interactions of them.

4.3. Homeostasis

Homeostasis is a steady state that regulates the keeping of state variables at a constant or stable condition. Homeostasis is defined as a closed-loop control system that balances changes of target values. Biological systems like human body struggle to control its internal environment against internal and external influences. If homeostasis is unsuccessful in the body, vital functions cannot continue to work and the system drifts into chaos. Almost all homeostatic control mechanisms involve negative feedback loop which provides long-term control to maintain a steady state. Negative feedback has a self-regulating mechanism for maintaining homeostasis. Negative feedback mechanism involves some important factors. The first one is sensor or receptor which senses changes in the system variables that need to be regulated. The second is a control center which has a set point or threshold value that keeps the optimal value of the system variable. The other is an effector which produces a response that eliminates or reduces the changes of the system variables. Negative feedback loop runs until the system variables are adjusted at optimum values.

There are many negative feedback control mechanisms in the biological systems. The human physiology is one of the best examples of the biological systems in which the negative feedback mechanisms are observed. Some negative feedback control mechanisms that occur in the human body include regulation of blood pressure, keeping the pH constant, regulation of oxygen and carbon dioxide concentration in the blood, hormonal regulation of blood glucose levels, thyroid regulation, the control of body temperature, etc.

In this chapter, an example of negative feedback control mechanism that occurs in the human body is presented with ABMS approach.

4.3.1. The control of the temperature: thermoregulation

In this case study [16], an agent-based homeostatic control model that regulates the body temperature during fever is presented. Fever is defined by an increase in body temperature above the normal range. Three types of agents, receptor agent, controller agent, and effector agents, are defined. Receptor agent is represented by thermoreceptor agent which senses changes in the body temperature. Controller agent has a set point which keeps the optimal value of body temperature. Effector agents are a set of dynamic autonomous agents which represent blood vessel that is a component of cardiovascular system [17]. Effector agents have been developed with ABMS approach [8]. The blood vessel is divided into segments. Each segment represents an agent. All of the agents in the negative feedback control mechanism are illustrated in **Figure 8**.

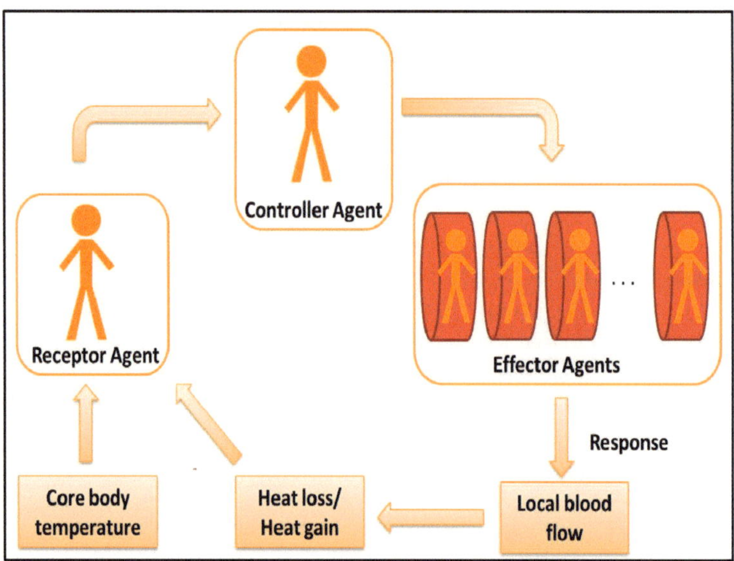

Figure 8. Negative feedback control mechanism of thermoregulation [16].

During the simulation runtime, each agent defined in the negative feedback control mechanism interacts with other agents. All of the agents interact with each other by using Java message service. Java message service supports "publish/subscribe" message delivery model. Receptor agent monitors the change of the body temperature and publishes it to the controller agent who has subscribed to the value. Controller agent receives message that includes the body temperature value. Controller agent compares the body temperature value to its set point value. Controller agent sends a message to the effector agents which start or stop the negative feedback mechanism. Effector agents produce a response based on the message that they receive, and they publish to the receptor agent to correct the deviation with negative feedback. Negative feedback control mechanism achieves a balance between heat production and heat loss. The output of the negative feedback mechanism is illustrated in **Figure 9**.

The simulation has a scenario of fever disease. This scenario achieves a balance with the agent-based negative feedback control mechanism as follows:

1. At the initial time, the core body temperature fluctuates between 36.7 and 37.2°C which is an acceptable normal range inside the human body. The set point of the body temperature is set to 37°C.

2. An infection that causes a fever disease is assumed that it starts with increasing the body temperature. The set point of the body temperature is set to 40°C at which the maximum value is assumed by homeostasis. The body temperature is less than the new set point of the body temperature.

3. Increased body temperature triggers shiver which is the reaction of the body. Shiver tries to gain the body heat which causes the constriction of the blood vessel called vasoconstriction. The controller agent publishes message "VASOCONSTRICTION" to the effector

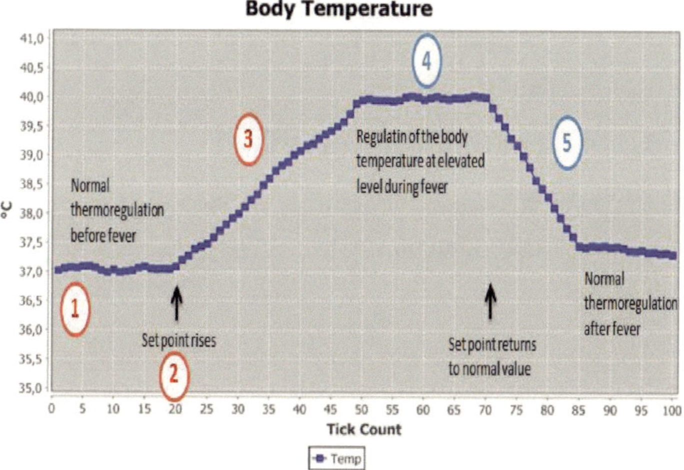

Figure 9. Regulation of the body temperature [16].

agents. The effector agents decrease their radius values to produce a response. Local blood flow parameter depending on the radius helps the heat gain.

4. The body temperature reaches the new set point of the body temperature. The infection is assumed to be cleared inside the body. The set point of the body temperature is set to 37°C. The body temperature is more than the new set point of the body temperature.

5. Condition at fourth step triggers sweat. Sweat tries to reduce the body heat which causes the dilation of the blood vessel called vasodilation. The controller agent publishes message "VASODILATION" to the effector agents. The effector agents increase their radius values to produce a response. Local blood flow parameter depending on the radius helps the heat loss. Thus, the body temperature returns to the optimal value.

In the result of this case study, it is observed graphically how the body temperature is regulated during fever. Agent-based negative feedback control mechanism can be called adaptation loop [18]. This is because the negative feedback control mechanism is run by a set of dynamic autonomous agents. In this mechanism, it is possible to observe their local behaviors.

5. Conclusion

This chapter has introduced the reader to ABMS, and it described implementations of different case studies utilizing the Repast Simphony toolkit. ABMS offers an extensible way to model biological systems consisting of autonomous and interacting agents which perform their actions and adapt their behaviors. Computer simulation helps the researcher to explore the behavior of a dynamic system. This chapter is concluded by observing interactions of real systems' components in the abstraction level.

Author details

Şebnem Bora[1] and Sevcan Emek[2*]

*Address all correspondence to: sevcan.emek@cbu.edu.tr

1 Ege University, Izmir, Turkey

2 Manisa Celal Bayar University, Manisa, Turkey

References

[1] Di Marzo Serugendo G, Gleizes M-P, Karageorgos A, editors. Self -Organising Software From Natural to Artificial Adaptation. London New York: Springer Heidelberg Dordrecht; 2011. 462 p. DOI: 10.1007/978-3-642 -17348-6

[2] DeAngelis DL, Grimm V. Individual-based models in ecology after four decades. F1000Prime Reports. 2014;**6**:39. DOI: 10. 12703/P6-39

[3] Borshchev A, Filippov A. From system dynamics and discrete event to practical agent based modeling: Reasons, techniques, tools. In: The 22nd International Conference of the System Dynamics Society (SDS'04); 25-29 July 2004; Oxford, England

[4] Macal CM, North MJ. Agent-based modeling and simulation. In: IEEE Proceedings of the 2009 Winter Simulation Conference (WSC); Austin, TX; December 2009. pp. 86-98

[5] Kluegl F, Bazzan ALC. Agent-based modeling and simulation. The AI Magazine. 2012;**33**:29-40

[6] Bonabeau E. Agent-based modeling: Methods and techniques or simulating human systems. Proceedings of the National Academy of Sciences. 2002;**99**:7280-7287. DOI: 10.1073/pnas.08080899

[7] Bandini S, Manzoni ST, Vizzari G. Agent based modeling and simulation: An informatics perspective. Journal of Artificial Societies and Social Simulation. 2009;**12**(4):4

[8] Bora Ş, Evren V, Emek S, Çakırlar I. Agent-based modeling and simulation of blood vessels in the cardiovascular system. SIMULATION. Special Issue, 2017. DOI: 10.1177/0037549717712602

[9] Macal CM, North MJ. Tutorial on agent-based modelling and simulation. Journal of Simulation. 2010;**4**:151-162. DOI: 10.1057/jos.2010.3

[10] Nianogo RA, Arah OA. Agent-based modeling of noncommunicable diseases: A systematic review. American Journal of Public Health. 2015;**105**(3):20-31

[11] Nikolai C, Madey G. Tools of the trade: A survey of various agent based modeling platforms. Journal of Artificial Societies and Social Simulation. 2009;**12**(2):2

[12] Crooks AT, Heppenstall AJ. Introduction to agent-based modelling. In: Heppenstall AJ, Crooks AT, See LM, Batty M, editors. Agent-Based Models of Geographical Systems. Dordrecht: Springer; 2014. pp. 85-105

[13] Ozik J, Collier NT, Murphy JT, North MJ. The relogo agent-based modeling language. In: Proceedings of the 2013 Winter Simulation Conference (WSC'13); 8-11 December 2013. pp. 1560-1568. DOI: 10.1109/WSC.2013.6721539

[14] Bora CB, Emek S, Kose H. Agent-based modeling and simulation of the sunn pest-what relation and of the struggle against sunn pest in Turkey. In: Proceeding of the International Conference on Engineering Technology and Innovation (ICETI'17); 22-26 March 2017. pp. 340-347

[15] Bora CB, Emek S, Evren V, Bora Ş. Modeling and simulation of the resistance of bacteria to antibiotics. Periodicals of Engineering and Natural Sciences. 2017;**5**(3):396-408. DOI: 10.21533/pen

[16] Bora Ş, Emek S, Evren V. An agent-based approach in homeostatic control systems: Thermoregulation. In: IEEE 9th International Conference on Computational Intelligence and Communication Networks; 16-17 September 2017. pp. 113-116. DOI: 10.1109/CICN.2017.8319367

[17] Guyton AC, Hall JE. Textbook of Medical Physiology. 11th ed. Amsterdam: Elseiver Saunders; 2006

[18] Salehie M, Tahvildari L. Self-adaptive software: Landscape and research challenges. ACM Transactions on Autonomous and Adaptive Systems. 2009;**4**:1-14. DOI: 10.1145/1516533.1516538

Modeling, Motion Study, and Computer Simulation of Thomas Earnshaw's Chronometer Detent Escapement Mechanism

Ivana Cvetković, Miša Stojićević and
Branislav Popkonstantinović

Additional information is available at the end of the chapter

http://dx.doi.org/10.5772/intechopen.79939

Abstract

The escapement is a very important horological invention and it is commonly used in theory of clocks and chronometers. It transfers energy to the timekeeping element and allows the number of its oscillations to be counted. The chronometer detent escapement used in marine chronometers was modified and simplified by Thomas Earnshaw, English renowned watchmaker, in order to make it available to the public. This chapter deals with 3D modeling and assembling of all escapement parts in SolidWorks, as well as constructive geometry of mechanism and computer simulation. The whole process has been accomplished in program "SolidWorks 2016," where all parts are assembled by using standard mates since this approach is suitable for motion and dynamical analysis. Generated simulation results are very close to the real ones, thereby using computationally strong kinematic solvers.

Keywords: computer simulation, escapement mechanism, Thomas Earnshaw, detent chronometer, motion analysis

1. Introduction

Escapement is a mechanism in mechanical clocks or watches, and it is considered to be one of the most important horological inventions. It transfers energy to the timekeeping element and allows the number of its oscillations to be counted [1].

The detent or chronometer escapement is considered the most accurate of the balance wheel escapements and it was used in marine chronometers [1]. In 1748, Pierre Le Roy invented the early form of it. He created a pivoted detent type of escapement [2, 3]. Around 1775, John Arnold invented the first effective design of detent escapement. In 1780, Arnold's escapement was modified by Thomas Earnshaw [3, 4]. If watches or clocks had been equipped with free harmonic oscillators, they would have performed harmonic oscillations with constant frequency. But real watch balance wheels always perform dumped and driven oscillations. Thomas's modification to the chronometer escapement was very close to previously mentioned ideal [5].

Two different but equally important functions are accomplished by escapement:

1. Impulsive: It maintains the balance wheel oscillations and keeps its amplitude constant [5, 6].
2. Regulative: It regulates the speed of the watch main movement [5, 6].

Important characteristics of Thomas Earnshaw's chronometer detent escapement mechanism are:

1. Balance wheel (oscillator) is almost free from the escapement influence and thus independent from the interference by the main gear train. In accordance to this, Thomas Earnshaw's escapement belongs to the escapement group named as "detached." Balance wheel coupled with detached escapement performs almost free harmonic oscillations [5].
2. Escapement wheel is locked on a stone (jewel) carried in a detent. Impulse is given by the teeth of the escapement wheel (when a tooth is unlocked) to a pallet on the balance staff in every alternate swing of the balance wheel. Instead as a pivoted lever, the detent is designed and constructed as a blade spring and consequently does not require lubrication [1, 5].
3. Geometry and kinematics of the escapement teeth and impulse pallet are designed in such a way that they also do not need lubrication. This feature is of greatest importance for the stability of the balance wheel oscillations and uniform chronometer's going rate [5].

2. Constructive geometry and basic principles

Figure 1 shows all components of chronometer escapement mechanism. Escapement wheel (1) receives the energy from twisted mainspring and is mashed with the last gear of the chronometer main gear train [5]. Balance wheel (B) performs torsion oscillations with a rotational motion about the axis of the helical spring (S), while the rotation of escapement wheel is blocked by the locking pallet (10) until the discharging pallet (5) pushes the gold spring (9) supported by the horn of detent (11) [5, 7]. Discharging event occurs during the period of time in which balance wheel (B) rotates in positive (counterclockwise) direction. As the

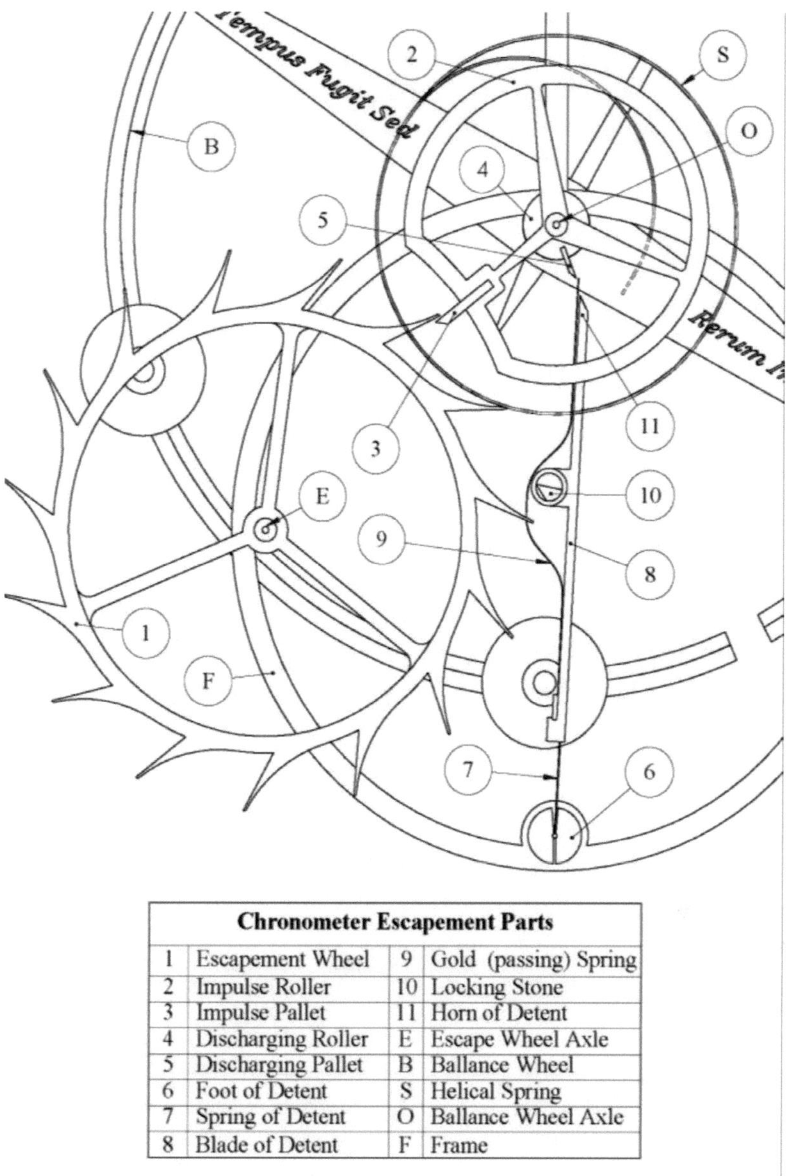

Chronometer Escapement Parts			
1	Escapement Wheel	9	Gold (passing) Spring
2	Impulse Roller	10	Locking Stone
3	Impulse Pallet	11	Horn of Detent
4	Discharging Roller	E	Escape Wheel Axle
5	Discharging Pallet	B	Ballance Wheel
6	Foot of Detent	S	Helical Spring
7	Spring of Detent	O	Ballance Wheel Axle
8	Blade of Detent	F	Frame

Figure 1. All parts of Thomas Earnshaw's chronometer detent escapement mechanism.

balance moves, the discharging pallet (5) on the balance staff engages the gold spring (9) and moves the detent blade (8) until the locking stone (10) releases the wheel tooth. At that precise moment, one tooth of the escapement wheel drops (escapes) and the next in advance engages the impulse pallet (3), which is a jewel fastened into the impulse roller [1, 5]. As the balance wheel proceeds, the wheel tooth continues to push the pallet (3), and after the short movement, the detent (8) is released and drops back to rest. Now, in the rest position, detent locking stone

(10) is ready to lock the nest tooth. The wheel tooth continues to push on the pallet (3) until the tooth drops off, and the appropriate tooth is locked on the detent locking stone (10) [5, 7]. On its return, the balance wheel (B) rotates clockwise and comes against the gold (passing) spring (9) through the discharging pallet (5) again but on the opposite site [2, 5]. However, as the balance wheel (B) proceeds, instead of lifting the detent (8), the passing spring (9) gives way, and as the balance continues rotation, the passing spring (9) is released. This is particularly important for the proper operation of the escapement since no push or impulse is given to the locking stone (10) and discharge roller (4) during the clockwise rotation of the balance wheel (B) [5]. Escapement working cycle can repeat endlessly long. This was the explanation of basic working principles of Thomas Earnshaw's chronometer detent escapement mechanism.

Some of the parameters of escapement constructive geometry (**Figure 2**) are known, some of them can be acquired willingly, and the rest must be rigidly established [5, 7].

Commonly, the escapement wheel has 15 teeth that are at mutual angular distance out of 24°, even though the wheels of 12, 14, and 16 teeth can be found often. The angle between *EO* and detent line is 45°, the diameter of escapement wheel is assumed to be d_E = 120 mm, and the

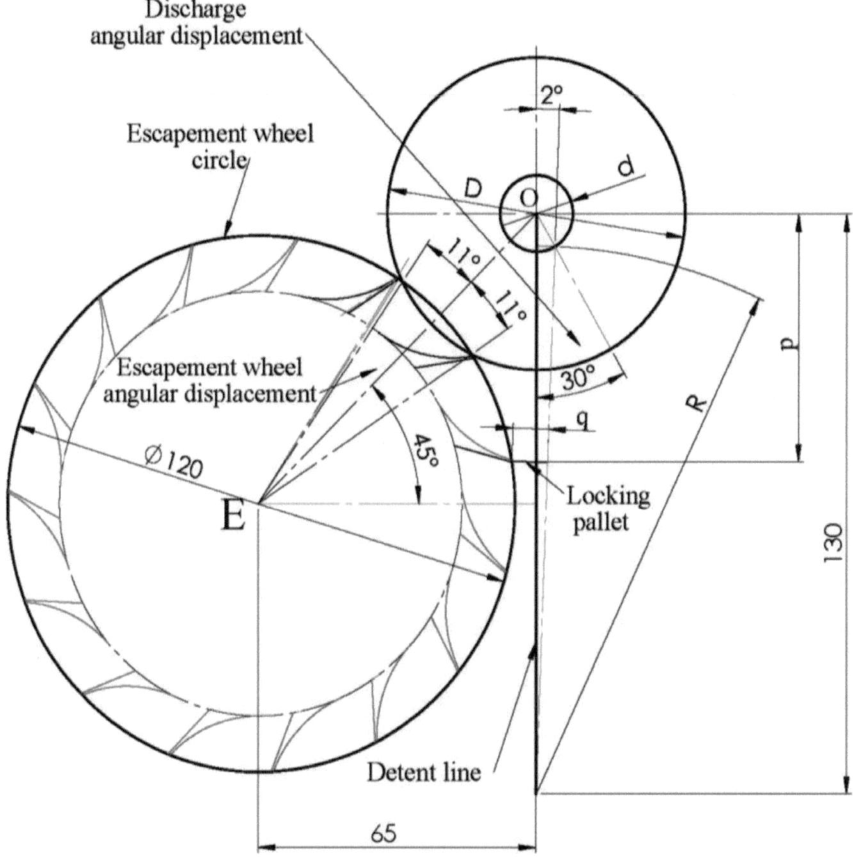

Figure 2. Constructive geometry of Thomas Earnshaw's chronometer detent escapement mechanism.

length of detent line is assumed to be l_d = 130 mm. The distance between the point E (center of escapement wheel) and detent line should be a bit longer than the radius of escapement wheel and it is presumed to be l = 65 mm. For the reason of safe mashing between impulse pallet and escapement teeth, the impulse pallet drop of at least 1° on each side of the pallet must be defined, and as a result, the escapement wheel rotates by 22° [5]. The diameter of the impulse pallet circle D_i is determined by geometrical construction in SolidWorks sketch, as well as D_d (diameter of the discharge pallet's circle—the assumption is that it rotates by 30° during discharge) and R (length of the detent—the assumption is that it rotates by 2° during discharge). The position p and length q of the locking pallet can be found from the disposition of the escapement tooth and detent angular displacement [1, 5].

There is no need for lubrication of the escapement wheel of Thomas Earnshaw's chronometer escapement and that is its biggest advantage over all other watch escapements. Balance's impulse pallet and the escape tooth roll together, so there is less friction (they not slide across one another) [2, 5]. Lubricant viscosity changes due to the temperature changes (it can even dry up), and the ability of chronometer escapement to run dry can result in more consistent timekeeper [5, 7]. The constructive geometry of this mechanism can be modified and adapted by dynamical analysis [5].

3. Making of 3D model and assembly

Since the constructive geometry and basic principles have been explained so far, now, 3D modeling can be easily conducted. Making of 3D model and assembly was completed in "SolidWorks 2016" and the procedure will be explained in continuance.

As it is known, when using some of the programs for 3D modeling, all parts of one assembly must be modeled separately. In this case, all parts of chronometer detent escapement mechanism were created according to the constructive geometry that is previously explained and applied in sketches definition. The set of SolidWorks commands named "Features" was used for part modeling. Commands such as "Extruded Boss/Base," "Revolved Boss/Base," "Lofted Boss/Base," and "Swept Boss/Base" were used for material adding, while commands such as "Extruded Cut," "Revolved Cut," "Lofted Cut," and "Swept Cut" were used to remove the material in various ways. Part modeling includes the specification of materials and physical properties that are principally important for dynamical analysis and appropriate motion study of a mechanism as a whole. **Figure 3** [5] shows the modeling of escapement wheel. All other components are modeled in the same way; they are shown in **Figure 4** and their list is given beneath:

1. Escapement wheel
2. Impulse roller
3. Balance wheel and discharge roller
4. Balance wheel thermal compensation

5. Helical spring
6. Gold (Passing) spring
7. Detent
8. Locking pallet (Jewel stone)
9. Discharging pallet (Jewel stone)
10. Impulse pallet (Jewel stone)
11. Chronometer mechanism frame [5, 8].

All parts named above have been assembled in one functional mechanism in accordance with kinematical principles and constructive geometry that has been previously explained.

Complex assemblies contain many different parts, which can be the components of some other assemblies, so-called sub-assemblies [5]. When adding a part to an assembly, the bond between them is made and when user opens the assembly in SolidWorks, one can identify the

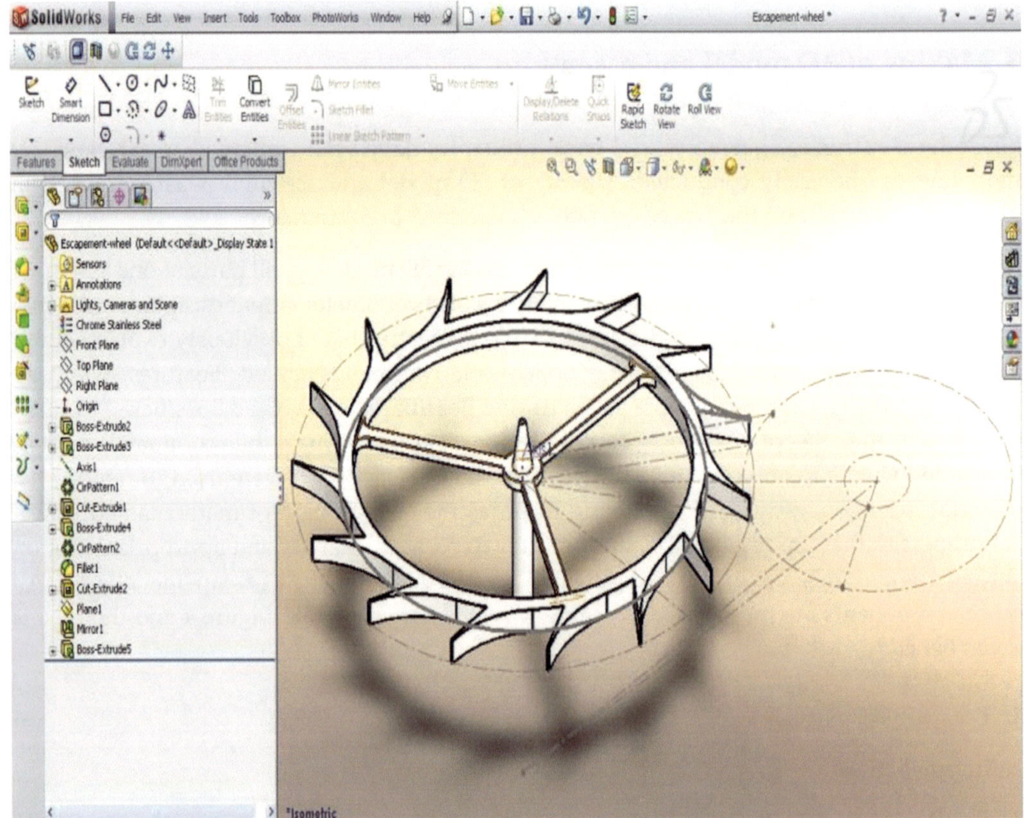

Figure 3. Escapement wheel modeled in SolidWorks 2016.

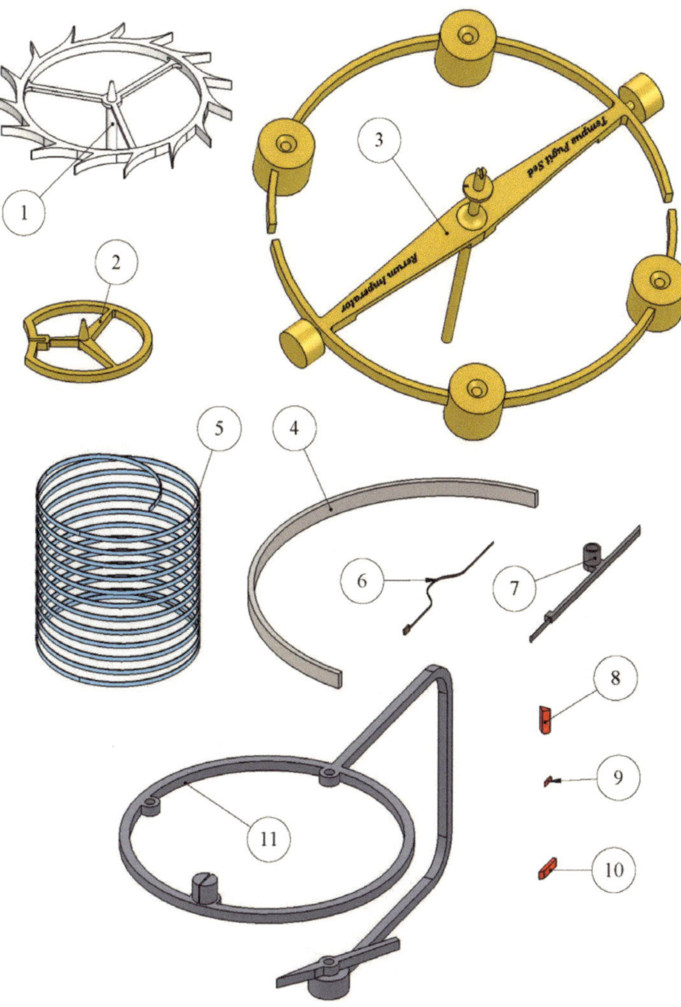

Figure 4. Components of chronometer detent escapement mechanism.

component file as a part of assembly. Changes in components manifest in the very assembly and parts are linked by command "Mate" that creates geometric tie between components. Mates define the allowable directions of linear or rotational motion of the components. They can be moved within its degrees of freedom, visualizing the assembly's behavior [8, 9]. Complete chronometer detent escapement modeled in "SolidWorks 2016" is shown on **Figure 5** [5].

There are three categories of mates—standard, advanced, and mechanical.

1. Standard mates define geometrical links between components (parallel, tangent, concentric, coincident, perpendicular, distance, or angle). For example, a concentric mate forces two cylindrical mates to become concentric, while a coincident mate forces two planar faces to become coplanar [8].

2. Advanced mates include limit, symmetry, width, path, profile center, and linear/linear coupler. For instance, profile center mate automatically center-aligns geometric profiles to each other and fully defines the components. A path mate constrains a selected point on a component to a path that has been defined by selecting one or more entities in the assembly [8].

3. Mechanical mates contain gear, screw, hinge, slot, rack and pinion, cam-follower, and universal joint mates. For example, a hinge mate limits the movement between two components to one rotational degree of freedom. Gear mates force two components to rotate relative to one another about selected axes. A cam-follower mate is a type of tangent or coincident mate and it allows the user to mate a cylinder, plane, or point to a series of tangent extruded faces [8, 9].

The assembling of Thomas Earnshaw's chronometer detent escapement was done only by using standard mates. This access describes the real process of the mechanism assemblage [5]. Firstly, chronometer frame is set as an immovable part of mechanism. Then, balance and escapement wheels are linked to the frame (axles of balance and escapement wheel are concentric with related bearings). On the inner surface of the balance wheel are thoroughly adhered two thermal compensation pieces. Helical spring is attached to the balance wheel and the frame (coincident mate is used), so its axis and axis of balance wheel are collinear. Detent assembly is made by linking detent blade to the detent foot so it can rotate about

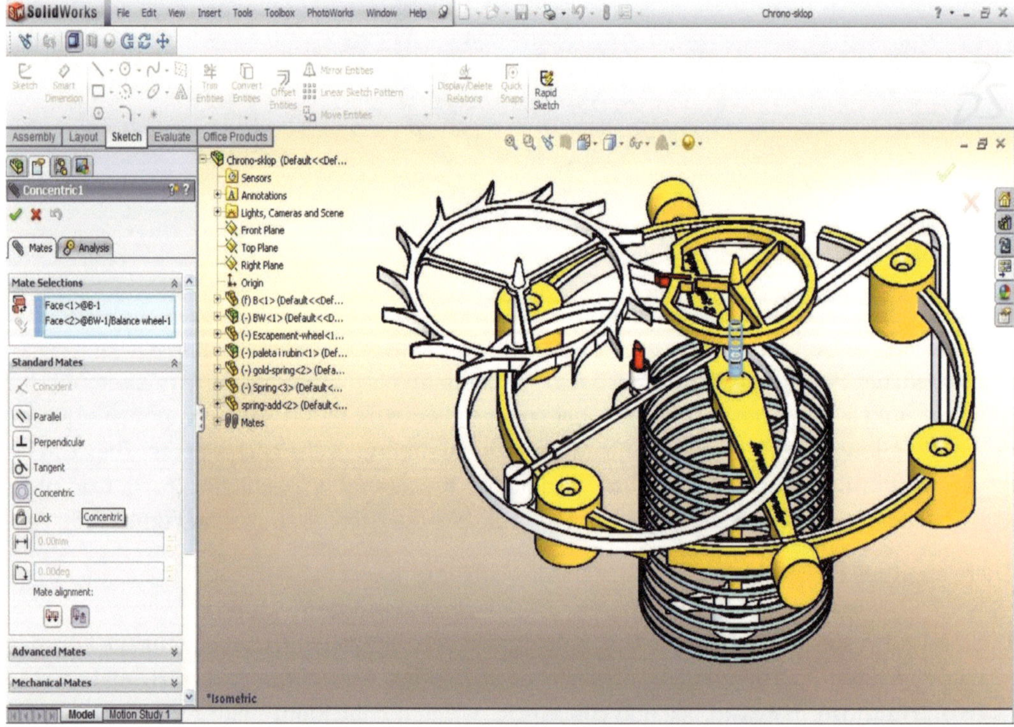

Figure 5. The assembly of Thomas Earnshaw's chronometer detent escapement mechanism.

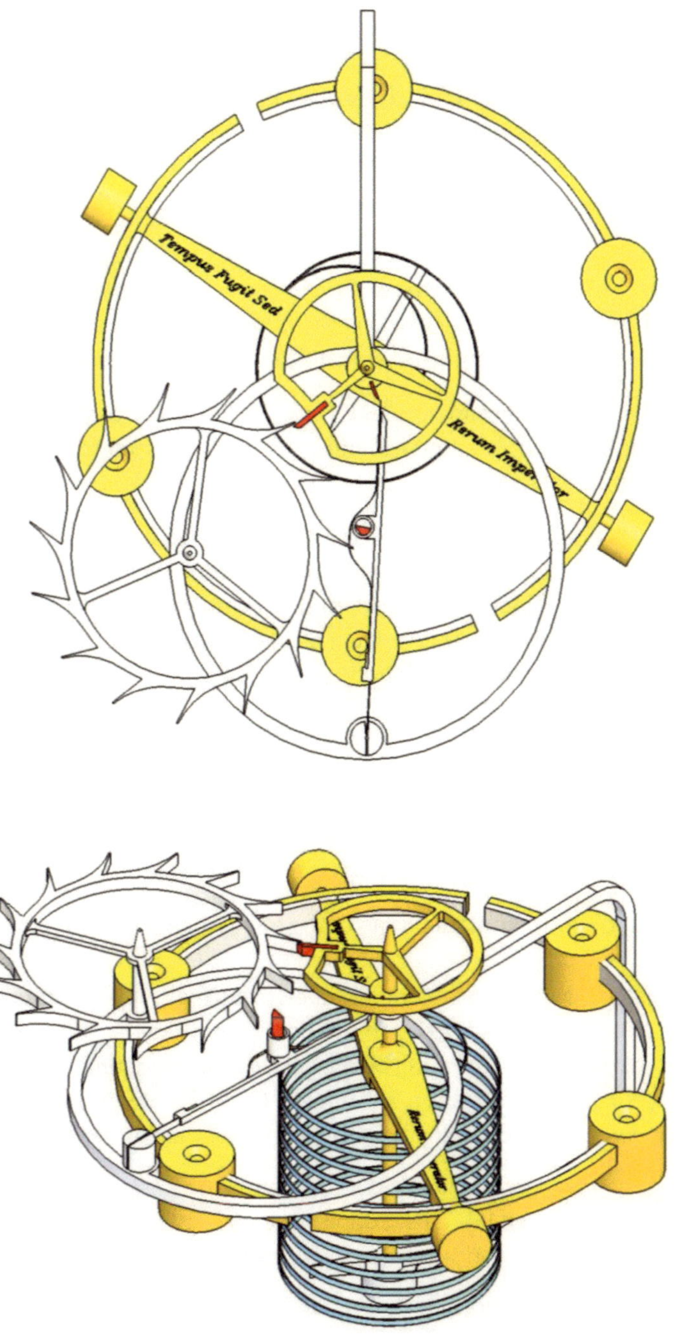

Figure 6. Horizontal and isometric projection of Thomas Earnshaw's chronometer detent escapement mechanism.

detent foot axle. Eventually, mechanism is completed by adding three pallets–the locking, the impulse, and the discharging jewel stones [1, 5, 8]. Chronometer detent escapement mechanism is shown in **Figure 6** in horizontal and isometric projection [5].

4. Motion study

SolidWorks motion studies are graphical simulations of motion for assembly models. Motion studies do not change an assembly model or its properties, but they simulate and animate the motion that is prescribed for a model. Motion study has a timeline-based interface named "Motion Manager" that includes animation, basic motion, and motion analysis [8, 9].

Animation is available in core of SolidWorks, and it can be used to animate the simple motion of assemblies by adding motors to drive the motion of one or more parts of an assembly or by prescribing the positions of assembly components at various times using set key points. Animation uses interpolation to define the motion of assembly components between key points [8].

Basic motion is available in the core of SolidWorks and it can be used for the approximation of the effects of motors, springs, contact, and gravity. Even though the mass is taken into consideration, computation is relatively fast [8, 9].

Motion analysis is available with the SolidWorks application "Motion TM" add-in to SolidWorks Premium. It is used accurately for simulations and analyses of the effects of motion elements (dampers, forces, springs, and friction) on an assembly. Motion analysis uses computationally strong kinematic solvers and accounts for material properties as well as mass and inertia in the computations [9].

The graphics section for SolidWorks motion study of Thomas Earnshaw's chronometer detent mechanism is split horizontally into upper and lower area and it is shown on **Figure 7** [5]. Assembly of the mechanism as a whole is in the upper area and the lower area is divided into three segments: timeline with key points and time bar on the right, the motion manager toolbar across the top, and the motion manager design tree on the left [5, 8, 9].

The motion manager toolbar contains some of the following property managers:

1. Gravity (property manager) is a simulation element that moves components around an assembly by inserting a simulated gravitational force. Gravity parameters are direction reference and numeric gravity value, but only one of these definitions can be used in any simulation [8, 9]. Gravity has been eliminated from dynamical analysis of escapement mechanism, since it does not affect the performance of the mechanism [8].

2. Damper (property manager) is consisted of linear and torsional damper and it simulates the effects of energy dissipation [8]. This motion study does not deal with dumpers separately, since the dumping characteristics have already been included into the spring simulation [5].

3. Motors are motion study elements that move components in an assembly by simulating the effects of various types of motors. Motors can be rotary and linear [8]. This function was not used in the motion study of Thomas Earnshaw's chronometer detent escapement mechanism [5].

4. Springs are simulation elements that move components around an assembly by simulating the effects of various types of springs. They can be linear and torsional springs [8]. Parameters are spring constant (k), damping constant (c), free length (angle ϕ), exponent

of spring force expression (*e*), and exponent of damper force expression (*d*) [8, 10]. Spring property manager was used for the simulation of helical spring (**Figures 4** and **5**), gold (passing) spring (**Figures 4–6**), and detent blade (**Figures 4–7**), and parameters settings for the simulation are shown in **Table 1** [5].

5. Contact must be defined in a motion study to prevent parts from penetrating each other during motion [8]. Forces can be generated between contacting components, or components can be constrained to touch continually [5]. In the motion study of this mechanism are shown four different contacts: between discharging pallet and gold spring, escapement wheel teeth and impulse pallet, detent, and gold spring and between escapement wheel teeth and locking pallet [5, 8]. Static and kinetic friction coefficients simulate dry friction, since the lubrication of escapement wheel teeth is not needed. The escapement wheel is made of steel and all pallets are made of ruby (corundum) [8, 9].

6. Force/Torque property manager applies forces, moments, or torques with uniform distribution to faces, edges, reference points, vertices, and beams in any direction for use in structural studies [8]. Forces can be defined by type, parameter values, and mathematical expressions [9]. The escapement wheel receives the energy from the twisted chronometer's mainspring and the constant torque out of $M = 25$ N acts on it [5].

The motion manager tree (on the left) is divided involves used simulation elements (forces, motors, and springs), components entities that appear in SolidWorks Feature Manager design tree, orientation, and camera views settings [9]. The timeline is located to the right of the motion manager design tree. It displays the times and types of animation events in the motion study and it is divided by vertical grid lines corresponding to numerical markers showing the time [8, 9].

Key points represent a beginning or end of a change in animation position or other attributes at a given time. In other words, a key point is the entity that corresponds to define assembly component positions, visual properties, or simulation element states. Key frame defines the portion of the timeline that separates key points (it can be any length of time). Change bars are horizontal bars connecting key points and they indicate a change between key points (component motion, animation duration, and simulation element property changes) [5, 8, 9].

As it was previously mentioned, standard mates were used for the assemblage of chronometer escapement components since these mates do not change physical properties of assembly in dynamical analysis.

The working cycle of Thomas Earnshaw's chronometer detent escapement mechanism is divided into six steps that are shown in **Figure 8** [5]:

1. Rotation of the escapement wheel is blocked by the detent locking pallet. Balance wheel rotates counter clockwise [5, 7].

2. Discharging event is taking place. Discharging pallet engages the gold spring and moves the detent blade until the moment when locking stone releases the wheel tooth [5].

3. Impulse event is starting to occur. Tooth of the escapement wheel drops (escapes) and engages the impulse pallet. The balance wheel proceeds counter clockwise, and the wheel tooth continues to push the pallet [5, 7].

4. The detent is released by the discharging pallet and drops back to rest. The escapement wheel tooth continues to push on the pallet until the tooth drops off, and the appropriate tooth is locked on the detent locking stone. Impulse event is finished. The balance wheel reaches its amplitude position and begins to rotate clockwise [5].

5. The balance wheel rotates clockwise and comes against the passing spring through the discharging pallet again, but on the opposite site. However, instead of lifting the detent, the passing spring gives way. As the balance wheel continues rotation the passing spring is released [5, 7].

6. The balance wheel reaches its amplitude position and begins to rotate counter clockwise. Mechanism has just finished the complete working cycle and is ready to repeat the new cycle, which is effectively equivalent to the previous one [7].

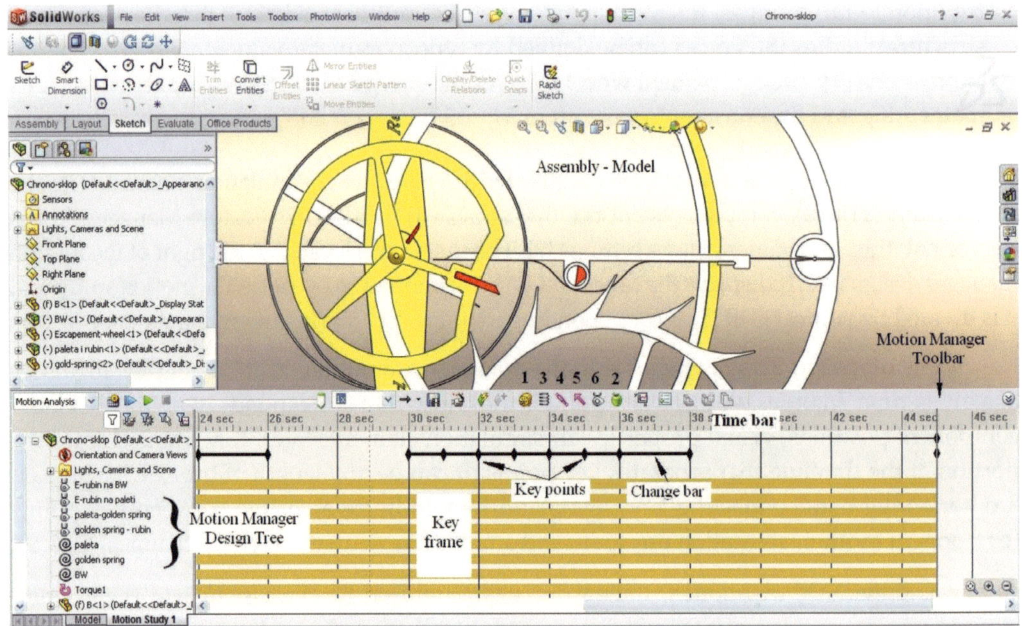

Figure 7. Motion study of Thomas Earnshaw's chronometer detent escapement mechanism.

	φ [deg]	k [mm/deg]	c [N mm/(deg/s)]	e	d
Helical spring	180	0.1	0.02	1	1
Gold spring	0	15.0	0.05	1	1
Detent blade	0	0.05	0.0001	1	1

Table 1. Parameters settings for the motion manager spring function.

http://dx.doi.org/10.5772/intechopen.79939

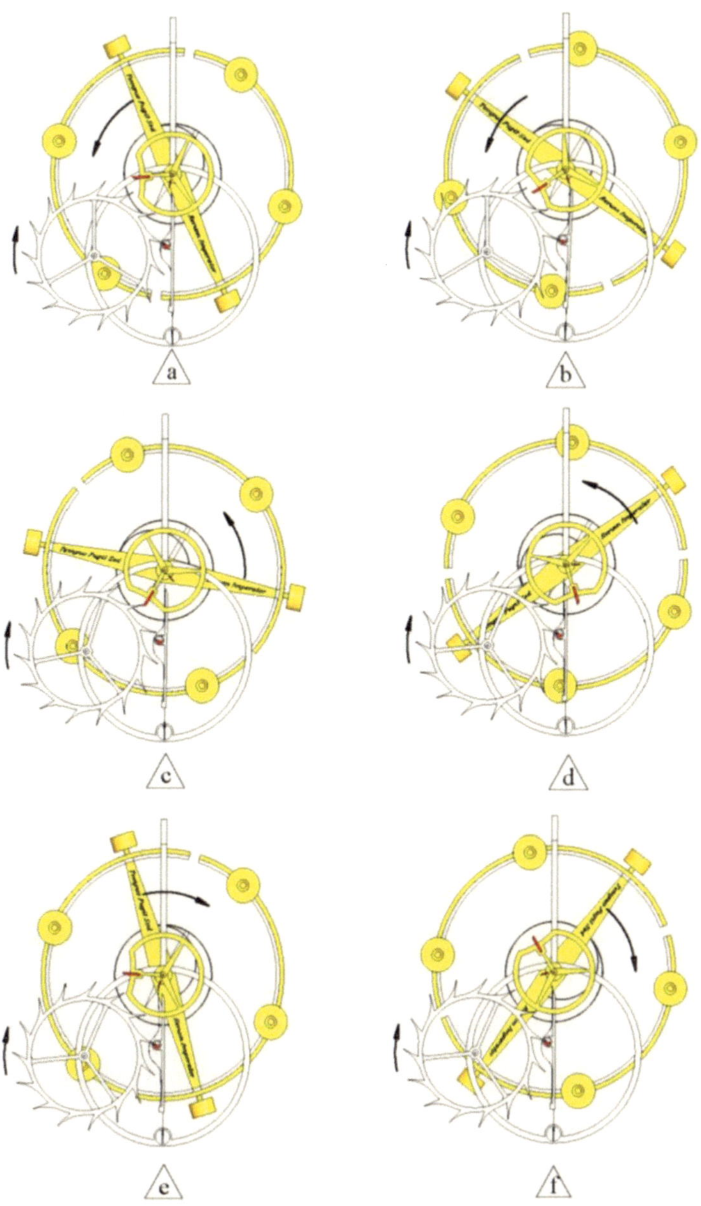

Figure 8. Six steps (a–f) of working cycle of Thomas Earnshaw's chronometer detent escapement mechanism.

The amplitude of the balance wheel oscillation must achieve the value of nearly 270° to each side of its center equilibrium position. This amplitude can be achieved by choosing the proper value of the escapement wheel torque [5]. The center equilibrium position should be chosen in such a way to deliver impulses to the impulse pallet symmetrically and that can be achieved by the adjustment of the helical spring free angle [1, 5].

5. Conclusion

This chapter deals with constructive geometry and basic principles of Thomas Earnshaw's chronometer detent escapement mechanism. Moreover, it deals with 3D modeling and assembling of previously mentioned chronometer, thus showing the whole process of making a mechanism and its motion analysis. Solid modeling, motion analysis, and simulation are done in "SolidWorks 2016" and they are based on constructive geometry that is explained at the very beginning. Even though the chronometer escapements are invented in the past times, these mechanisms present the basis of today timekeepers' industry.

Author details

Ivana Cvetković*, Miša Stojićević and Branislav Popkonstantinović

*Address all correspondence to: ivanacvetkovic1992@gmail.com

Faculty of Mechanical Engineering, University of Belgrade, Belgrade, Serbia

References

[1] Anonymous. Watch and Clock Escapements—A Complete Study in Theory and Practice of the Lever, Cylinder and Chronometer Escapements, Together with a Brief Account of the Origin and Evolution of the Escapement in Horology. Worcestershire, UK: Read Book Ltd; 2017. p. 186

[2] Daniels G. The Practical Watch Escapement. London, UK: Philip Wilson Publisher; 2013. p. 82

[3] Macey SL. Encyclopedia of Time. Abingdon, UK: Routledge; 1994. p. 726

[4] Woodward P. My Own Right Time. New York: Oxford University Press; 2003

[5] Popkonstantinovic B, Obradovic M, Malesevic B, Jeli Z. Solid modeling and motion study of chronometer detent escapement mechanism. Volume: Buletinul-Institutului Politechnic Din Isai Sectia 5 Sonstructii De Masini, ICEGD 4th International Conference; Iasi, Romania; 2011. pp. 55-72

[6] Matthys RJ. Accurate Clock Pendulums. New York: Oxford University Press; 2004

[7] Ruxu D, Longhan X. A brief review of the mechanics of watch and clock. In: The Mechanics of Mechanical Watches and Clocks. History of Mechanism and Machine Science. Vol. 21. Springer, Berlin, Heidelberg; 2013. p. 5-45. DOI: 10.1007/978-3-642-29308-5_2

[8] Tickoo S. Solidworks 2016 for Designers. 14th ed. CADCIM Technologies; 2016

[9] Chang KH. Motion Simulation and Mechanism Design with Solidworks Motion 2016. SDC Publications; 2016. p. 152

[10] Rusov L. Mehanika III – Dinamika, Naucna knjiga. Naučna KMD, Belgrade, Serbia: Beograd; 1994. p. 427

Chapter 5

The Role of Computer Simulation Tools in Improving the Quality of Life in Small Settlements of the Czech Republic

Vojtěch Merunka

Additional information is available at the end of the chapter

http://dx.doi.org/10.5772/intechopen.81244

Abstract

This chapter presents the computer-aided organisational modelling and simulation of relevant socio-technical processes with regards to the new housing and building law and regional management trends in the European Union. We present an example related to the processes and agendas of the urban planning of the landscape areas and small settlements. Our models were simulated, verified and validated to help the officials (especially from the smallest settlements) to improve their knowledge to allow them to participate more in the future. As one of the dimensions of quality of life is the self-realisation and participation of local people, we expect an improvement in the quality of life in general. Our approach uses the novel type of process maps, which describe the legislation, visualise it and simulate it. These models consist of the original combination of FSM and object-orientation. It gets local people a better understanding of their life situations without the need for thorough prior training. It also causes the effect of better participation and subsequent improvement of the quality of life, because of the actual and specific problem in the Czech local government of small settlements in the low level of participation of citizens in these small villages caused by the complexity and also time-varying form of law and statutory regulations.

Keywords: BORM, FSM, object-orientation, business process simulator, EU legislation, regional management, building law, e-democracy, participation of citizens, quality of life

1. Introduction

We have to answer problems related to the small settlement development and enlargement, landscape care and overall efforts to improve the quality of life and the level of democracy while

preserving the conditions of the sustainable development (addressing living standard, cultural and historic value, agricultural and industrial production, transport infrastructure construction, tourism potential, etc.). Technophobia of local people significantly increases this problem because the low-level knowledge of local people is strongly contrasting with high knowledge of external people and (owners and investors for example) penetrating the rural area, who use good information and communication technologies (ICT) (especially geographical information systems and project management) and process management knowledge.

Business process models show the collaboration of more participants within the solved system. They also can be visually animated in case of need to teach participating people their roles. We need this approach for simulation, validation and verification of the real world problems from the area of agriculture, landscape management and country planning. A fundamental purpose of such a business model is to create and simulate a complex interconnected system, where local actors, citizens, regional government, various interested organisations and partners and other participants mutually communicate. In addition to that, business process models are also the foundation of subsequent system modelling activities of software engineering, organisational design and management consulting. The typical method of performing these activities is to start directly by drawing process maps without performing the initial interviews. However, we present the idea, which for better modelling, we need to use a specific textual technique, which helps us to recognise, define and refine our initial set of business process participants and their properties before performing any graphical modelling activity.

In our experience, any modelling and simulation diagramming technique or instrument aimed for some real and practical projects should be intelligible to the stakeholders who are not typically well educated in ICT. Furthermore, these models must not inadequately simplify or distort requirement information. We recognised that the correct visualisation of the problem into the model and subsequent optional simulation is a challenging but essential task for standard diagramming techniques. We believe that the business community still lacks a powerful yet easy-learned tool for process modelling; capable of performing a comparable function to that operated by Flow-Charts, Entity-Relation Diagrams or Data-Flows Diagrams over the past decades. One of the strengths of these old techniques and tools was that they included only a restricted set of concepts (about 5) and were understandable by problem domain professionals after few minutes of learning. Regrettably, Unified Modelling Language (UML) and Business Process Model and Notation (BPMN) approach lost this advantage of clearness and simplicity.

2. Motivation

Czech landscape development suffers from the low level of inhabitants' participation in small settlements of rural areas. We examined to model and visually simulate process-based knowledge about legislation about the urban planning and building development to obtain visual simulation an instrument for increasing the participation of local people in activities related to their real-life situations.

We have recognised that there is a low level of knowledge about participation possibilities in business and workflow processes of territorial planning and development. According to several political declarations by the European Union like Spatial Planning Charter and Aarhus agreement by the European Council, we have to accept that ICT has potential to resolve the low level of local people participation, which decreases their quality of life.

The expected result of modelling and simulation activities is represented by structured data (tables, lists, forms...) that can be directly used as an instrument for knowledge improvement or implementation of some systems or an organisational change in the way of management consulting services. This is why there are the following main dangers described by [1, 2]:

1. *inability*—some important details cannot be expressed due to the deficiency of used method.
2. *oversimplification*—we are forced to simplify the modelled subject while trying to finish its visualisation.

3. Organisation modelling

The organisation modelling is a necessary ingredient for the start of the whole system development life cycle. Darnton [3] and Taylor [4] say that the main obstacle (defined from the perspective of the software application development) with this step of the requirement analysis of socio-technical systems stands in the early steps of the whole system life cycle. The first step of any modern approach should contain two steps. The first one is the designation of the requirements in the form of business processes and their participants. The second one is the formation of a model, often called an essential object model or business object model, developed as a set of domain-specific subjects and participants known as essential elements. These two steps should be completed with the active participation of the domain experts, because they are able to guarantee that the accurate model will be made. Obviously, every modelling tool used at these early stages should be intelligible to the domain experts, because they are typically not skilled in ICT. Furthermore, these instruments must not damage or badly simplify requirement information.

The most used approach for business-process modelling in current object-oriented methodologies is use case modelling as the origin of the documentation process in UML. Jacobson founded the concept of use cases in the early 1990s [5]. The principal information source on UML is the website [6]. Ambler [7] says, use cases are usually the basis of most object-oriented development methods. Use case modelling consists of the identification of actors, which are external subjects communicating with the software section of the modelled system.

It is our experience that the accurate description of the system boundary is a troublesome duty, which usually needs deep knowledge of the proposed system, which must be included in the phase of system requirements specification. Some insufficiencies in this approach are stressed in Barjis [8]. There are miscellaneous opinions on the reasonability of use cases and similar instruments in the first phase of system modelling. Simons and Graham [9] very well explained examples where use case modelling could destroy the true logic and system behaviour. Unfortunately, standard UML-based tools are too oriented at the software engineering and programming logic, but there are yet another approaches for business modelling:

1. Many other process modelling tools are based on Petri Nets. The advantage of this method is that it is both graphical and has a solid mathematical basis. The best implementation of Petri Nets is the event-process chain (EPC) diagram from Aris methodology [10].
2. Other approaches use diverse species of flowcharting. This method is the oldest graphical technique practised in computer science. It was originally used for visualising the sequences and control of computer program instructions. Nowadays, flowcharts are often used to express details of business logic. A very good application of flowcharts is workflow diagram applied in Proforma Workbench or FirstStep Business CASE Tools. Of course, it is also a sort of the activity diagram of UML [11] and a quickly expanding standard Business Process Model and Notation (BPMN, http://www.bpmn.org/).
3. The third approach used here is the use of automata finite-state machine (FSM). FSM has a solid theoretical background ([12] for example), as well as Petri Nets. A practical implementation of state machines is the state-chart diagram in UML, for example. Certainly, the sequence diagram of UML also includes some behaviour of FSM.

The overview of all approaches for simulation business processes described here is presented in **Table 1**.

Approach	Theory behind	Advantages	Disadvantages
EPC–Aris	Petri Nets	Very popular in Europe, has Aris CASE Tool, easy and clear method for domain experts.	Little link to possible subsequent software development techniques, slow analysis, low expressiveness of large models.
UML activity diagram or BPMN	Flowchart	Industry standard, has many CASE tools with Unified Modelling Language (UML) or Business Process Modelling Notation (BPMN).	Too much computer based, difficult to understand by domain stakeholders.
UML Sequence Diagram and State Diagram	Finite State Machines	Industry standard, has many CASE tools with Unified Modelling Language (UML).	Too much computer-based, difficult to understand by domain stakeholders.
Workflow Diagrams	Flowchart	Easy and clear method for domain experts, perfectly has many business CASE Tools.	Little link to possible subsequent software development techniques, obsolete method.

Table 1. Most used simulation approaches.

4. Our Solution—BORM as the FSM and OOP combination

Our expertise in system modelling recommends that classical UML is not proper for the initial steps of analysis, where business processes must be identified. UML diagrams are too complicated for the users from the problems domain community as they oftentimes include extreme detail concerning possible software implementation. This involves classes, inheritance, public/private methods, attributes, link classes, etc. Nearly the same practice we have is written in Simone and Graham [9].

We conclude that the business community requires an easy but powerful tool for business process modelling and simulation; capable to perform an equivalent function to that performed by Entity-Relation Diagrams, Data-Flows Diagrams or Flow-Charts known in the past. One of the advantages of these timeworn tools was that they included only a little set of concepts (typically not more than seven), which caused them intelligible by business experts after a very short learning time. Regrettably, UML and BPMN method missed this power.

That is why we developed our own Business-Object Relation Modelling (BORM) process diagram and our own way to start business system analysis. The initial work on Business-Object Relation Modelling (BORM) was carried out in 1993 under the support of the Czech Academic Link Programme (CZALP) of the British Council, as part of the *Visual Application Programming Paradigms for Integrated ENvironmentS* (VAPPIENS) research project; further development and recent practical projects in the last decade has been supported by the Craft.CASE Ltd.—the British software consulting company supporting innovative technologies. (*VAPPIENS was financed by the British Governments CZALP, managed by the British Council. The authors acknowledge the support they received from this source, which enabled them to meet and carry out the initial work, out of which BORM grew.*)

Our approach is founded on the reclaim of old thoughts from the early 1990s concerning the modelling of object features and behaviour by automata (FSM). The first book articulating the potential blend of the Object-Oriented Approach and Finite-State Automata was the Shaler's and Mellor's [12]. Taylor [4] wrote one of the best books speaking about the applicability of OOP to the business modelling. These early works together with our practical experience is the reason why we believe that the business requirement modelling and simulation and software modelling could be unified on the background of object-oriented approach and automata theory.

Figure 1 shows an example of a model of a book in a library characterised in a form of an automaton having three phases: a book on a shelf, a book on loan and a returned book to be put back on a shelf. These phases are easily recognisable through an interview with domain experts. When these phases are recognised, it is possible to identify behaviours required for transferring books between the states. Of course, other entities in the system can be also modelled as another automata, which mutually communicate to each other. Let us have a borrower as an example. Even they have their own phases, which can be related to the time-related situations of the book; and analogically, the borrower's behaviour can be related to the book's behaviour, see **Figure 2**. This figure shows that a satisfied borrower is associated

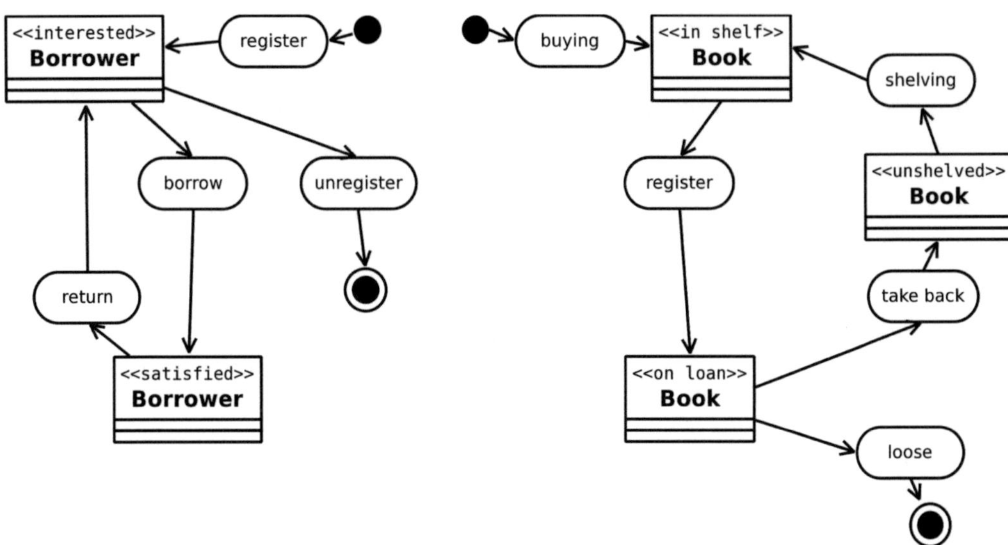

Figure 1. A book and a borrower as two FSM.

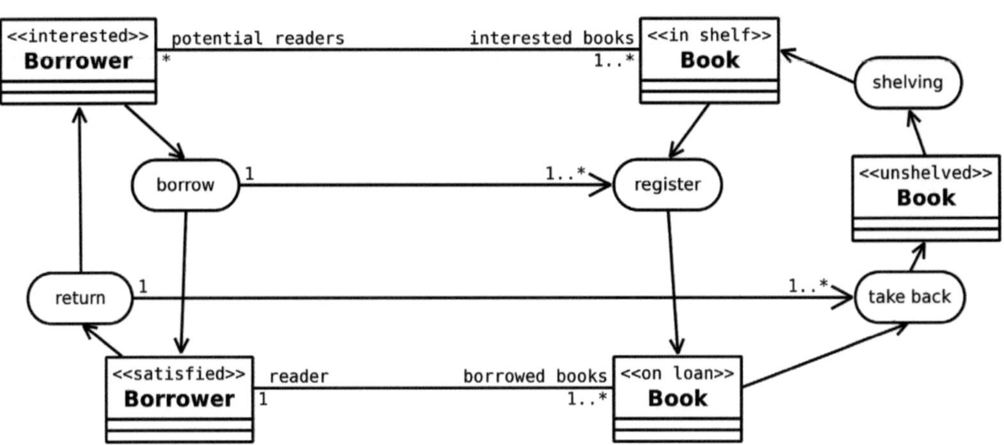

Figure 2. Two FSM mutually connected.

with an object of a book on loan in a relationship with cardinality of a 1 to many. That means, that every book on loan has to have its borrower and every satisfied borrower is satisfied if and only if he has at least one book borrowed. This is the possible business situation of our model. Similarly, we can identify the associations between borrower interested in borrowing a book and available books in the shelves. This association can be another possible business situation of our model.

Our given modelling approach unifies UML-manner of object modelling and business process modelling manner. Models like UML, BPMN and other can be easily derived from this BORM model. The proposed unified method unifies and simplifies object modelling. **Figure 3** presents the mapping of our model to the regular BPMN and **Figure 4** presents the same model represented by the state-chart of the regular UML.

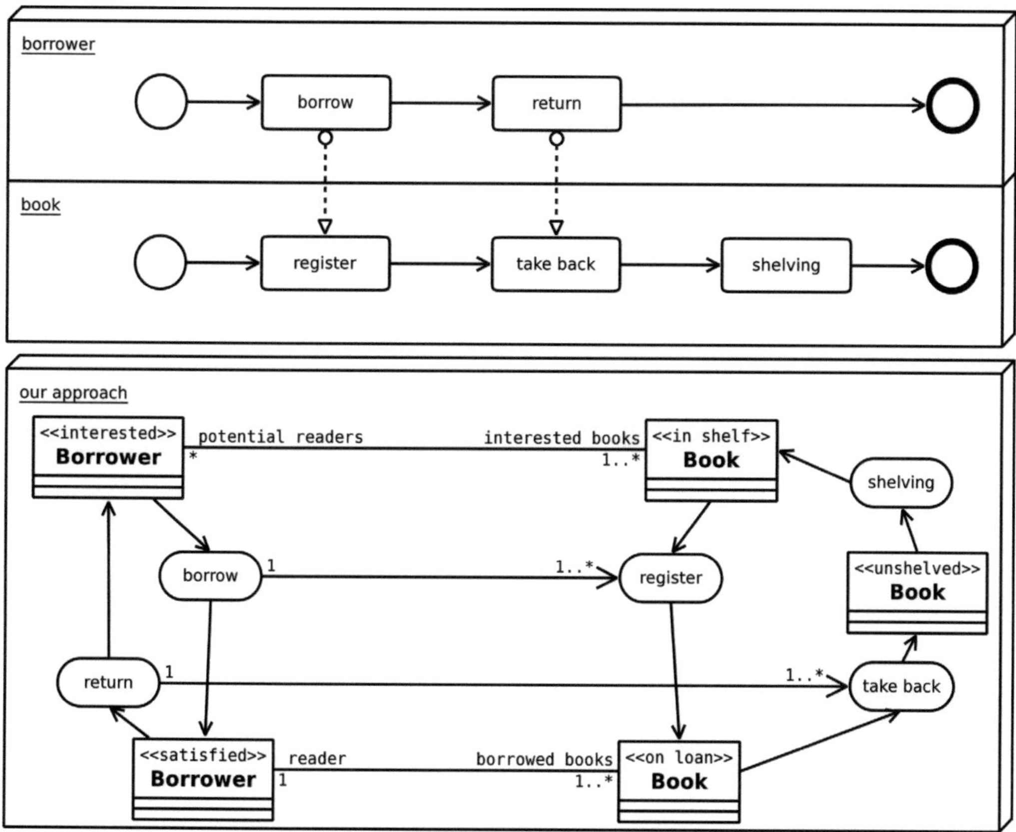

Figure 3. BORM and BPMN.

In our method, the states of objects are the most important elements. Behaviours denote only the necessary linkage between them. Both business processes and software components should be consequently modelled by starting with their states—situations of participating objects in the requested system in some moment. Modelling can be simpler, more correct and less behavioural imperative than it is now. Moreover, our focus on situations matches the conventional description of life situations, as is known above all from descriptions of the implementing regulations and the various guidelines, decrees and laws.

Likewise [3], we think that activities are key elements of business process modelling. Eeeles and Sims [13] describe a business process having a number of elements; activities, transitions, states and decisions. They assert that the UML activity diagrams can be a helpful modelling instrument in recording business processes.

In the organisation modelling, subsequent simulation is important that every participating object should be described as an automaton (FSM) with states and transitions dependent on the behaviour of other objects. Each state is defined by its semantic rule over object data associations and each transition is defined by its behaviour, necessary to transform the object from its initial to its terminal state. All organisational and business process models should be able to be simulated in this way. Hence, it should accent the mutual relationships (communications and associations) of states and transitions of objects in the modelled system.

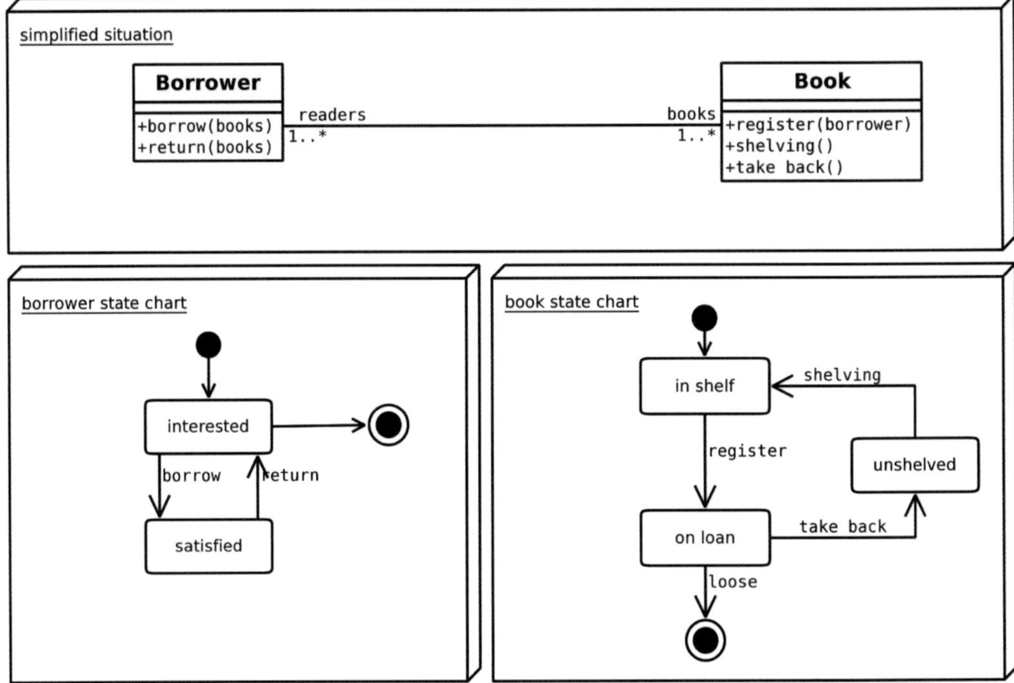

Figure 4. BORM model decomposed into standard UML models.

BORM has been used for a number of large projects by Deloitte consulting company, Central Europe office in Prague, including

- the identification of business processes in Czech health care system,
- the modelling of characteristic features of the Central European general agricultural commodities wholesale sector,
- business-process reengineering approach of the electricity supply industry,
- business-process reengineering approach of the Central-European telecommunication network management, and
- at last but not least, the project on improving the quality of life in small settlements of the Czech Republic which this text is about.

5. BORM in detail

5.1. Object-orientation

The object-oriented paradigm comes from the 1970s, when started the research of new species of user-friendly operation systems, graphical user interfaces and consequently in related programming techniques necessary for their software implementation. It changed software engineering paradigm by incorporating non-traditional ways of thinking into the field of applied computer science. On OOP, the software system is modelled as an abstraction of the real world in the very similar way as it is in classical philosophy (e.g. models, meta-models, ontologies, objects...). The basic building concept is an object that incorporates both data structures and their functionality. Another modelling approaches handle data and behaviour independently, but OOP is based on their mutual dependency. OOP has been and still is explained in many books, but we consider that this early work [14] written by OOP pioneers is still the best.

5.2. Finite-state machines

In the field of theoretical informatics, the finite-state machines (FSM) theory is a study of abstract automatons and the problems they can save. An automaton is a mathematical model for an entity that responds to its external environments, receives data and produces another data. Automata can be constructed in a way that the output from one of them becomes input for another. Finite-state machine activity is determined not only by receiving data but also by an internal status of given machine. The output is created as the combination of an input and internal status. For example, the FSM theory is essential not only for the computer science and engineering, but also for a human language translation theory. It has been explained in

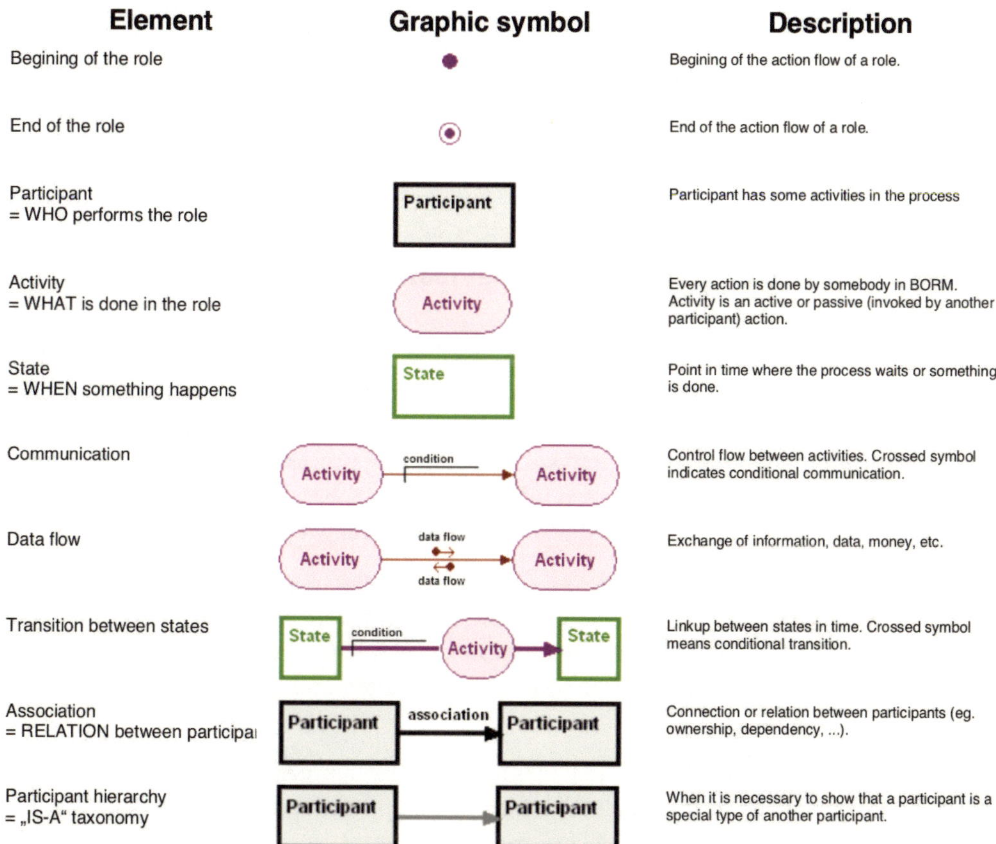

Figure 5. BORM business diagram symbols.

[12] and many latest publications. The idea of FSM also inspired behavioural features of the Unified Modelling Language [6].

5.3. BORM business diagram

BORM uses an original diagram for business process modelling and subsequent simulation (see **Figure 5**). It conveys together information from three separate UML diagrams: state, communication and sequence.

The BORM group has found that it is clearly understood by business stakeholders. Main principles of the BORM process diagram are:

1. Each subject participating in a process is displayed in its states and transitions.
2. This diagram expresses all the possible process interactions between process participants. The business process itself consists of a sequence of particular communications and data flows among participating subjects.

Officially, BORM process diagrams are graphical representations of interconnected Mealy-type automata, where each automaton represents some participating entity of the entire business process. The idea of modelling participating entities as FSM automata was firstly discussed in [12]. Visual simulation of a business process is based on market-graph Petri net. It is a very similar method, which is fully explained in [15]. Hence, we can model states, transitions and operations of all entities involved in a given business process in a very powerful but still relatively simple and intelligible graphics for domain experts who typically are not educated in detailed computed science.

6. BORM simulation models in regional management

Latest BORM application of organisational modelling and simulation was the project of enhancing the decision-making of mayors and people from local administration. It offered the possibility to model and simulate real-life situations in small settlements. The project activities were for modelling; simulation and reengineering processes related to the regional government processes of small towns and villages, and the subsequent development of supporting information systems addressing life situations of local people.

Today, we have to deal with many troubles related to the settlement expansion into the open landscape. We need to improve the quality of life and the level of democracy of these people while preserving the conditions of the sustainable development (attending living standard, historic and cultural values, agronomic production, building and maintenance of transport network, touristic value, etc.).

Urben sprawl described by Frumklin in [16] is an issue that our method can also resolve. The root of the urban sprawl in the small settlement development is the circumstance that the elected local people (e.g. clerks, politicians, mayors...) cannot be completely knowledgeable in every part of law and local government itinerary and their practical impacts on their settlements and their citizens. They do not know how to fully use the legislation in favour of the settlements and usually depend on a misleading interpretation provided by their governing bodies and more often by another subjects, who are frequently privately involved in the process in question and thus biased.

Urban sprawl an uncontrolled expansion of certain kind of urban build-up into the free landscape caused by favourable land prices, demand for cheap but modern estates, etc. Dualny and others wrote [17] about harmful absorption of original small settlement structures, which causes many negative effects. It is a wrong experience that arose in the second half of twentieth century in the advanced industrial countries (USA, France and Great Britain) and lately also in our country. At the beginning, citizens of affected settlements typically perceive the urban sprawl optimistically, mostly because of the lobbying.

We examined the legislation and local officials' experience related to the processes and agendas of the urban planning of the landscape areas and small settlements with regards to the new housing and building law and regional management trends in the European Union. It consisted of a series of simulation sessions with four business process models correlated to the building development and territorial planning. One of them is also our example of the process of building permission in **Figure 6**.

Our method handling business process models of EU-legislative and their visual simulation encourages the officials (particularly in the smallest villages) to explain this legislation and shows the possible alternatives of its use. Our models and their visual simulations explain how the BORM can be applied to improve the process of decision-making on the level of mayors and local officials. It allows the opportunity to model and simulate real-life situations in small villages. The example at **Figure 6** presents the BORM business object diagram of a process of acquiring building permits. **Figure 7** presents the particular step of Craft.CASE simulation software [18], where the BORM model can be visually step-by-step animated.

Our method is based on business-process models and their visual simulation. This helps the participating subjects (especially in the smallest villages) to explain the legislation and designates the optional ways of its performing. Our models and their visual simulation illustrate how it can be practised to improve the decision-making process on the level of mayors and local authorities. It makes the opportunity to model and simulate real-life situations in small villages. Our modelling software allows analysing particular simulation steps. Our diagram is a visual representation of object associations and communications within given business-process. Our notation is the re-used UML notation from the state diagram, activity diagram and sequence diagram UML but combined and simplified in an original way into a new diagram that shows the process in the manner of mutually interacting automata (FSM). Furthermore, we can use a visual simulator for animating these business processes. Our visual simulation software has incorporated the user group communication component inspired by Facebook chatting (see **Figure 8**).

Sure, when presenting our method, the target staffs are typically not educated in any ICT-related skill (Yet if they are people from small villages). On the other hand, the process-mapping stage must be fast accomplished. This is why the analysis team does not have much

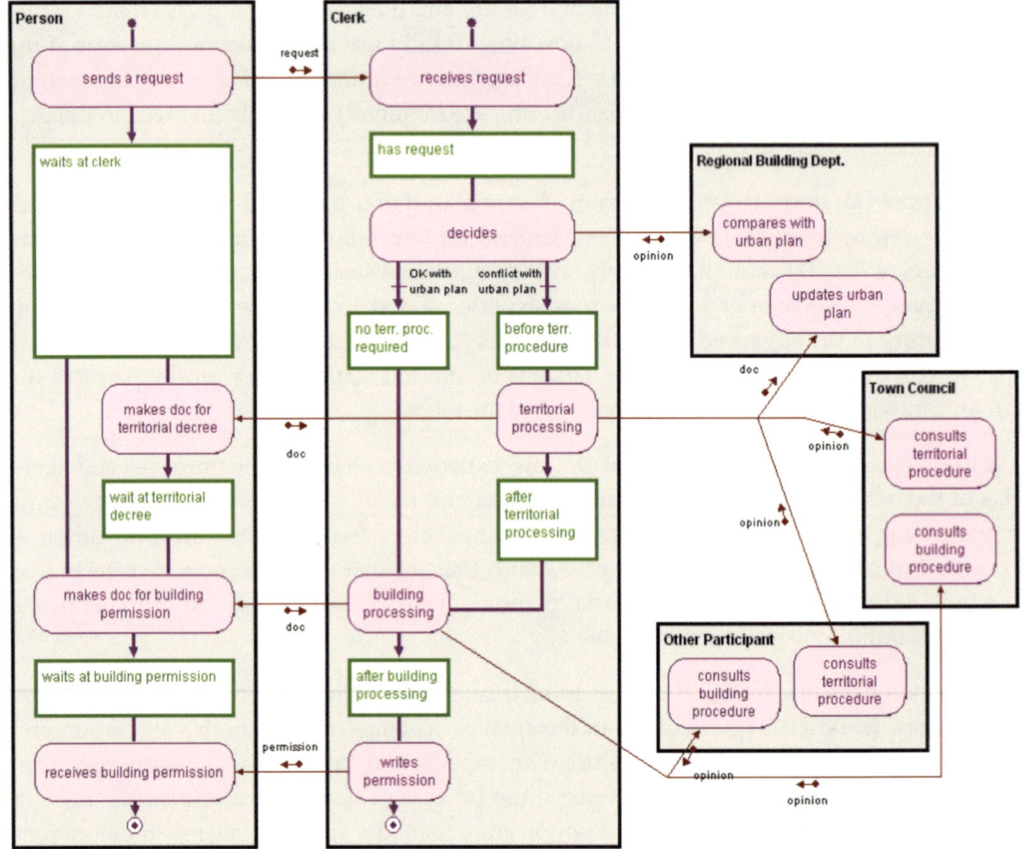

Figure 6. Building permission process.

time for detailed modelling training such as the explanation of all aspects of the used method with outcomes into the computer programming. Long-time education with a modelling software is also inapplicable. We typically have time only for a very short opening session on how to read our computer models. Here, we consider the big advantage of our method because this very introductory session typically takes only 20 minutes of a showing of how it works. Most people were ready to start their work after this primer.

Consequently, we identified that the ICT equipment is not a big barrier to use our method as we expected on the assumption that the people were from small villages.

We prepared our models in the professional modelling software Craft.CASE and then transported them to the environment of a freeware simulator, which is fully available via the fast Internet. The network was not a problem, because the Central Bohemian region, where we did our project, due to the vicinity of Prague (capital city of the Czech Republic) is adequately equipped with high-speed Internet.

Finally, we asked 57 people from the local government of several Central-Bohemian small settlements about the increase of their knowledge and about their evaluation of their past

http://dx.doi.org/10.5772/intechopen.81244

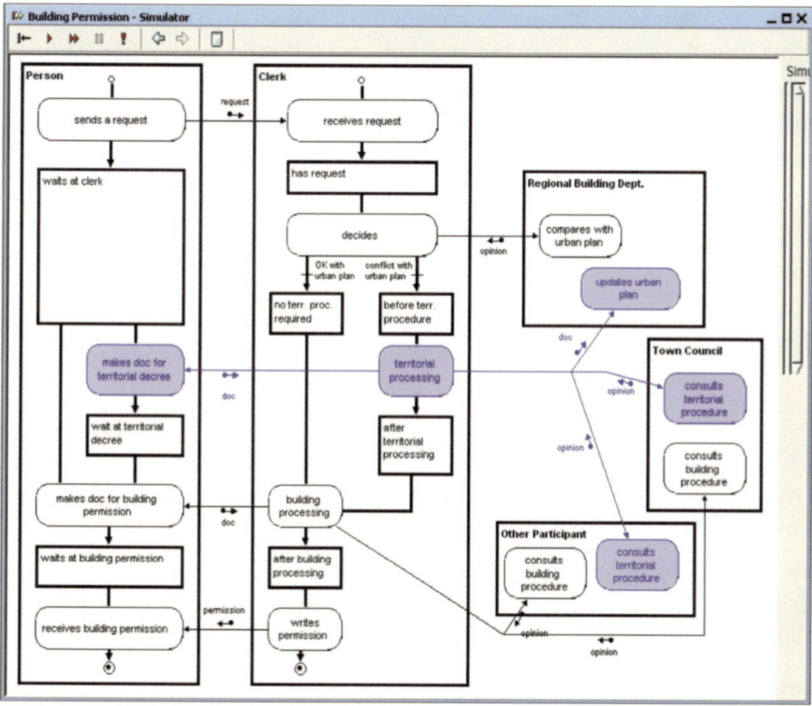

Figure 7. Step-by-step simulation in Craft.CASE tool.

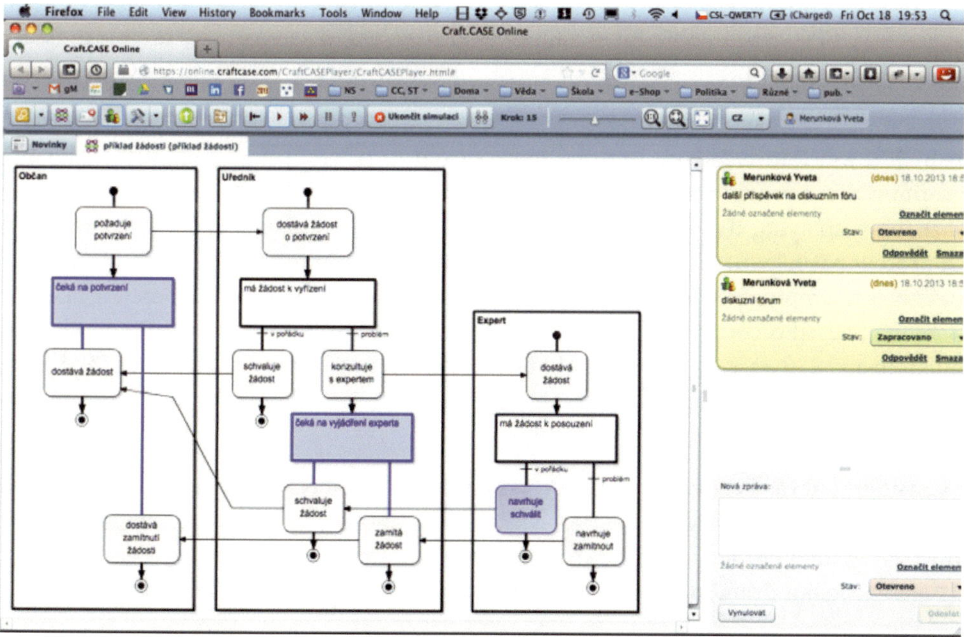

Figure 8. On-line BORM business process simulation of Internet user group.

projects from the attitude of the newly obtained information. The probability between the answer about the efficiency of our new method and the estimated better participation was 64%. Furthermore, based on the new information, 67% of tested people stated the evidence, that external investors and lobbyists manipulated them in the past due to their former low level of business-process knowledge.

Our conclusions are also worthy of the possible subsequent software development of information systems addressing better life situations of local participants.

7. Conclusion

The BORM method is built on the blend of the object-oriented approach with automata (FSM) and our working experience with the business modelling projects, which were intended to support the teams composed by business experts and software developers from various areas of socio-technical systems. We conclude that this method can improve the expected possible convergence of BPMN and UML models and support problem domain specialists in the area of organisation structures simulation as it is prognosticated by Scheldbauer in [19].

BORM is an object-oriented and process-based analysis and design method, which is proven to be effective in the construction of business systems. The effectiveness of BORM is based on its ability to record and display the fundamental features of the relevant business model, which can be simulated, verified and validated for subsequent software implementation. Furthermore, many partners in our projects work with diverse legacy Process Modelling Systems (e.g. EPC-based ARIS, for example). Nevertheless, these partners favour to analyse and design business processes using BORM and then rewrites these processes into their legacy method.

Our BORM innovation is based on the reuse of old ideas from the beginning of the 1990s concerning the representation of object-oriented subjects and their behaviour by automata (FSM) and displaying the process-based knowledge as the automata communication where each process participant is represented by own automaton. In the BORM method, states and situations are emphasised in distinction to activities as it is in standard process diagrams. We assume, based on our practical experience, that the business requirement modelling and simulation and software modelling could be unified on the platform of OOP and FSM, where objects (e.g. process participants described as Mealy-type FSMs) are interconnected via passing messages to achieve necessary behaviour.

We consider that the best value of BORM is caused by the specific way of modelling, which covers two different worlds: business engineering and software engineering. Moreover, BORM is an intelligible instrument for mutual communication between system architects and problem domain experts via organisation structures modelling and subsequent simulation.

Author details

Vojtěch Merunka

Address all correspondence to: vmerunka@gmail.com

Department of Information Engineering, Faculty of Economics and Management, Czech University of Life Sciences Prague, Prague, Czech Republic

References

[1] Igen D, et Hulin CL. Computational Modeling of Behavior in Organizations–The Third Scientific Discipline. Washington DC: American Psychological Association; 2000. ISBN 1-55798-639-8

[2] Aalst van Der W. Business Process Simulation Revisited, Keynote Speech at the EOMAS Workshop 2010 [cit: April 10, 2011 http://www.eomas.org]; 2010

[3] Darnton G, et Darnton M. Business Process Analysis. Cengage Learning Emea; 1997. ISBN 1-861-52039-5

[4] Taylor DA. Business Engineering with Object Technology. John Wiley; 1995. ISBN 0-471-04521-7

[5] Jacobson I et al. Object–Oriented Software Engineering–A Use Case Driven Approach. Addison Wesley; 1991. ISBN 0-201-54435-0

[6] The UML Standard, OMG – The Object Management Group. http://www.omg.org; ISO/IEC 19501

[7] Ambler S. Building Object Applications That Work, Your Step–By–Step Handbook for Developing Robust Systems Using Object Technology. Cambridge University Press & SIGS Books; 1997. ISBN 0521648262

[8] Barjis J. Developing executable models of business systems. In: Proceedings of the ICEIS–International Conference on Enterprise Information Systems. INSTICC Press; 2007. pp. 5-13

[9] Simons AJH, et Graham I. 30 Things that go wrong in object modeling with UML. In: Kilov H, Rumpe B, Simmonds I, editors. Behavioral Specifications of Businesses and Systems. Kluwer Academic Publishers; 1999. pp. 237-257

[10] EPC – Event-driven Process Chain. http://en.wikipedia.org/wiki/Event-driven_process_chain

[11] Fowler M. UML Distilled: Applying the Standard Object Modeling Language. Addison Wesley, Reading Mass; 1997

[12] Shlaer S, et Mellor S. Object Lifecycles: Modeling the World in States. Yourdon Press; 1992. ISBN 0136299407

[13] Eeles P, et Sims O. Building Business Objects. New York: John Wiley & Sons, Inc.;1998

[14] Goldberg A, et Rubin K. Succeeding with Objects–Decision Frameworks for Project Management. Addison Wesley; 1995. ISBN 0-201-62878-3

[15] Barjis J, et Reichgelt H. A petri net based methodology for business process modeling and simulation. In: The proceedings of the Fourth International Workshop on Modeling, Simulation, Verification and Validation of Enterprise Information Systems (MSVVEIS), Paphos Cyprus; 2006. ISBN 972-8865-49-X

[16] Frumkin H et al. Urban Sprawl and Public Health: Designing, Planning, and Building for Healthy Communities. Island Press; 2004. ISBN 978-1559633055

[17] Dualny A. Suburban Nation: The Rise of Sprawl and the Decline of the American Dream. North Point Press; 2001. ISBN 978-0865476066

[18] Craft.CASE Simulation Tool http://www.craftcase.com

[19] Scheldbauer M. The Art of Business Process Modeling–The Business Analyst Guide to Process Modeling with UML and BPMN. Sudbury MA: Cartris Group; 2010. ISBN 1-450-54166-6